Florida's Great Ocean Railway

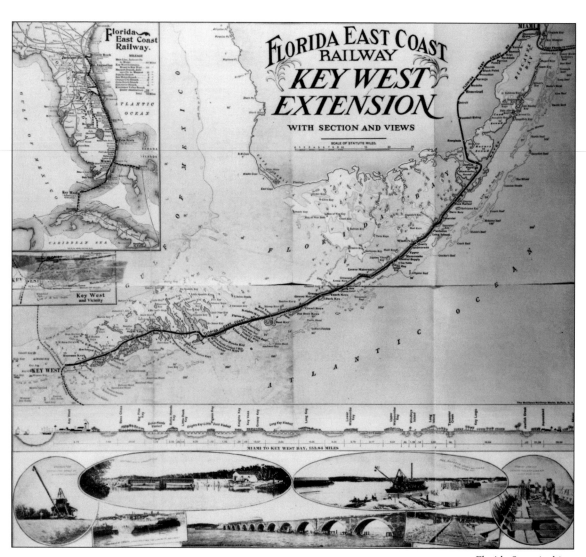

Florida's Great Ocean Railway

Building the Key West Extension

Dan Gallagher

Pineapple Press, Inc.
Sarasota, Florida

Inquiries should be addressed to:

Pineapple Press, Inc.
P.O. Box 3889
Sarasota, Florida 34230

www.pineapplepress.com

Library of Congress Cataloging-in-Publication Data

Gallagher, Dan, 1945-
    Florida's Great Ocean Railway / Dan Gallagher.
       p. cm.
Includes bibliographical references.
    ISBN 1-56164-269-X
    1. Florida East Coast Railway--History. 2. Railroads--Florida--Florida Keys. I. Title.
TF25.F58 G35 2003
    625.1'09759--dc21

                                                                2002014148

First Edition
10 9 8 7 6 5 4 3 2 1

Design by Shé Sicks
Printed in the United States of America

Contents

About This Book

BETWEEN 1905 AND 1916, the Florida East Coast Railway built a 128-mile extension from the mainland of Florida at Homestead south and west to Key West. The feat was remarkable in a number of ways. By the time it was completed, engineers had filled in more than twenty miles between the Florida Keys and built bridges over seventeen more miles of open water. They had moved nearly eighteen million cubic yards of sand, marl, and rock, using strong backs and clever machines of their own design. During this construction period, there were generally four thousand workers "down in the Keys" at any given time pitting their energy against a hostile environment. About 160 men died on the project, 120 of them in a single day.

Their story is told with pictures and graphics as much as with words. Nearly three hundred old photographs and figures help the reader visualize the scope of the project. These photographs have come from a number of collections, and most have never been published elsewhere.

It was a magic time for amateur photographers. By 1900, cameras were in the hands of the common person. They were simple to operate, fairly reliable, and often used by professional engineers as a hobby. For these reasons, there are a lot of photographs of the Key West Extension under construction. Some of these photos were taken to show or demonstrate techniques to other engineers, but most were taken for fun by these hobbyists. Consequently they are often of amateurish quality and not well framed or focused. Although a number of photos in this book are less than perfect, I've included them because of their uniqueness and their importance in explaining a process.

This book is fondly dedicated to the memory of Wright Langley
January 10, 1935 – August 12, 2000

WILLIAM WRIGHT LANGLEY LOVED PHOTOGRAPHY and old photographs. During his life in Key West, first as a reporter for the *Key West Citizen* and later as Key West bureau chief for the *Miami Herald*, Wright began what is possibly the largest private collection of old Keys photographs in existence. These spawned his early books, *Yesterday's Key West* and *Yesterday's Florida Keys* (both with Stan Windhorn). In later years, Wright and his wife, Joan Knowles Langley, wrote *Key West: Images of the Past, Old Key West in 3-D*, and *Key West and the Spanish American War.*

Wright and Joan formed the Langley Press in 1982 to ensure the continued publication of these and other local pictorial histories. Their work opened up avenues to preserve material that would have otherwise been lost. As with his work as director of the Historical Florida Keys Preservation Board, Wright understood that history not only needs to be preserved, it must also be made available for anyone interested to learn about it. Wright did more than save great chunks of Keys history: he gave it back to the people with his books.

Wright and Joan encouraged me considerably several years ago when I published my first book. I owe them both thanks for that. Wright contributed about twenty photographs to this book before he died. I only wish that he were here to be one of the reviewers.

Acknowledgments

WHILE I HAVE COLLECTED MATERIALS from dozens of sources in Florida, there are several special collections and resources that need to be mentioned. I am grateful to the following people:

Jerry Wilkinson, who had the foresight to preserve more than 1,500 newspaper clippings and magazine articles amassed by the Krome family that give specific dates for the F.E.C. activities. Jerry provided me with copies of all of these materials.

Bill Robinson, a Flagler railroad buff (and Amtrak engineer) who has collected plentiful materials on the F.E.C. Among his contributions to this book are copies of all of the annual construction reports of the F.E.C.and a copy of Hawkins' diary, as well as many good ideas.

Todd Tinkham, an early Key West Extension historian, who provided a number of photographs and deep insight into the project with his dissertation.

Ed Swift III, of Historic Tours of America, who gave me access to his personal and corporate photography collection. This includes a series of pictures from Miriam Reyburn-Steele, granddaughter of Harry Alfred Steele, a construction engineer whoe took a number of important photos in this book.

Tom Hambright of the Monroe County Library in Key West, who has wonderful knowledge of both the Keys and the Extension project, as well as the largest known collection of photographs detailing the bridge construction.

Wright Langley of Key West, who collected and shared historic information about the Florida Keys for many years. Thanks to Wright, many of the photographs in this book were brought back to the Keys from afar. Wright freely shared his knowledge and these photos for this book.

Dee Lloyd, executive director of the Museums at Crane Point Hammock, who graciously shared more than seventy photographs from that collection. These pictures, many also in the Krome collection, were documented and annotated by James H. Worrell, who donated them to the museum several years ago.

Karen Becker, Marathon, FL, who assisted with research on F.E.C. accidents and deaths.

Additionally, I'd like to give special thanks and credit to historical reviewers Seth Bramson, Bill Robinson, Irving and Jeanne Eyster, Jim Clupper, Joan Langley, Edwin O. Swift III, and Jerry Wilkinson, and to editors Marta Vanderstarre, Rita L. Irwin, and R. D. Irwin.

A Note about Photo Credits

The author wishes to thank the following institutions and individuals who contributed photographs to this work. All photos are acknowled-ed in the text as coming from the following sources:

Charles "Pete" Bow, private collection, Ocala, Florida
Seth Bramson, private collection, Miami, Florida
Historical Museum of Southern Florida archives, Miami, Florida
Wright Langley, private collection, Key West, Florida
Monroe County Public Library archives, Key West, Florida
Museums at Crane Point Hammock archives, Marathon, Florida
Albert Perez, private collection, Miami, Florida
Brian Schmitt, private collection, Marathon, Florida
Curtis Skomp, private collection, Key West, Florida
Steele—contributed by Mrs. Miriam Reyburn-Steele. In private
    collection of Edwin O. Swift III, Key West, Florida
Todd Tinkham, private collection, Marathon, Florida
Jerry Wilkinson, private collection, Tavernier, Florida
Calvin Winter, private collection, Miami, Florida

1

The Plan

THE MOST AMBITIOUS CONSTRUCTION project in the world during the first decade of the twentieth century was the great canal across Panama. The second-largest project—the Florida East Coast Railway Key West Extension—similarly captured the attention of the U.S. and international public. When the project began in 1905, engineers estimated that the line could be completed in eight years. But due to hurricanes, mosquitoes, unanticipated problems, and the

Fig. 1. The Long Key Viaduct. By the time the Extension was finished, the engineers had built nearly 18 miles of bridges. (Al Perez)

Fig. 2. Henry Morrison Flagler. (Monroe County Public Library)

sheer logistics of building 128 miles of railroad over the ocean, it took seven years to connect Key West to the rest of America and four more years to finish the project. At times there were more than four thousand construction workers in the Florida Keys engaged in the miserable tasks of moving millions of cubic yards of rock, clearing thousands of acres of jungle, hot-riveting steel under the subtropical Florida sun, and building immense concrete viaducts that still stand today as monuments to this great achievement. This book tells the story of the Key West Extension.

The project was the brainchild of Henry Morrison Flagler, a wealthy visionary and former partner of John D. Rockefeller of the Standard Oil Company. Flagler used much of the wealth he had amassed to build luxury hotels and a transportation system to link the hotels together. The Florida East Coast Railway and the Key West Extension to this line were his pet projects. He began the Extension when he was seventy-four years old.

Fig. 3. Construction workers in the Keys, 1906. (Museums at Crane Point Hammock)

The Florida East Coast Railway (F.E.C.) was not a newcomer to railway construction, nor was it afraid of large projects. The division had built roadway and laid track down the ocean coast of Florida during the last decade of the nineteenth century. The line reached Miami in 1896, and the city of Miami was incorporated in that same year. While this was a difficult task because of the rugged Florida jungles and swamps, getting track down from Jacksonville to Miami and to Homestead was not nearly as difficult as laying the last 128 miles from Homestead to Key West. The construction engineers had to embrace new technology to bridge the Keys and had to build a whole new set of construction tools for the project.

At that time, Florida was a state blessed with an extensive coastline but few sites that could berth oceangoing steamers. In 1890 the only ports with sufficient water depth were at Jacksonville/St. Augustine, Tampa Bay, and Key West. Florida, wealthy with sunshine, fresh water, and excellent year-round growing conditions, could not transport fresh produce to markets in the North. Thus the initial impetus for building the F.E.C. was to provide rapid transportation for agricultural products that could be grown in frost-free south Florida. Flagler also owned an extensive hotel chain and saw profit in extending the chain down the sunny coast, a venture that would succeed only with good transportation in place. A rail line would also open Florida up for settlement and development, both worthy goals at the turn of the century, goals that would justify the great expense of putting down the track.

As early as 1886, Flagler considered building a railway to Key West, but it was mentioned only casually. It was not until the road reached Miami in 1895 that the subject came up again. Even at that time there were no firm plans. In 1902 the F.E.C. initiated surveys of potential routes. Many critics held that the Extension could not be built and, if so, would never pay for itself because of the great investment it would require. They termed the project "Flagler's Folly." But in Flagler's dream, if the Key West Extension could be completed, the F.E.C. would have a terminal in the southernmost city in the U.S. accessible by both steamer and rail. Key West would be the closest U.S. port to the soon-to-be completed Panama Canal and would sit at the crossroads of all shipping to Cuba and the Caribbean. Key West was also strategically sited on the Gulf Stream near major shipping routes to the central portion of the U.S. These were sound reasons to consider the Key West Extension project.

Fig. 4. Old map showing the potential routes for water transportation from Key West.

Henry Flagler was in close touch with every facet of the planning and construction. He and his staff studied the project for two years before they made any decisions. J. R. Parrott, president and general manager of the F.E.C., often consulted with Flagler and with engineers as surveys and estimates came in. According to folklore, the following conversation took place between Flagler and Parrott in 1903:

"Can the road be built?" asked Flagler.

"It can," replied Parrott.

"Then go ahead and build it."

With these terse orders, Parrott brought together a few of the finest construction engineers in the U.S. for the project. They were to do the impossible: build the most ambitious rail line ever attempted, the railroad that went to sea. All of the work was to be done by the F.E.C. itself.

The success of the project hinged on available money and a good plan. Henry Flagler, one of the wealthiest men in America, had plenty of money and growing wealth from his successful Florida East Coast Railway and hotels. The engineering team, led by Construction Engineer James C. Meredith, provided the plan. It was a good plan because, while every mile of the railway was carefully drawn out, there was room in the plan for change if it became necessary. The original plan called for one long railway to be built on solid causeways or concrete viaducts over the entire route. This plan changed as the engineers learned about the difficulty of building concrete viaducts in deep water. The plan changed again as they decided to trade off construction speed and expense for long-term maintenance considerations. Fortunately, the plan was flexible enough to adapt to the realities of hurricanes, changing prices for construction materials, and Henry Flagler's health.

The Route: Overview

The route finally chosen was simple—begin the 128-mile rail line at Homestead, where track had been completed at the end of July 1904. After overland surveys of routes from Miami to Key West via the southern Everglades and through the Keys, F.E.C. engineers determined to proceed south from Homestead, cross twenty miles of sawgrass and swamp, and put in a bridge at Jewfish Creek to reach Key Largo. From this large key, they would take advantage of the relatively higher and firmer ground down through the Keys. They would have to cross three major bodies of water, one seven miles long, another thirty feet deep. The third major bridge, connecting Long Key with Conch Key, would have to be built early in the project in order to get to the halfway point at Key Vaca. Once at Key Vaca (actually Knight's Key Dock), the F.E.C. would be able to use the Extension in commercial service while continuing construction to Key West.

A number of locations became important as target sites for planning and temporary camps. Some of these were special because they were close to water routes, others because they afforded space and staging areas.

Miami Terminal Docks

The Miami Terminal Docks (located between Sixth Street and Ninth Street in Miami today) were the jumping-off point for the Extension construction project. Meredith and the project team had their administrative offices at this site in 1905, and they ran the project from Miami until March 1909, when the control center moved south to Marathon.

Prior to the beginning of the Extension project, the Miami Terminal Docks housed a machine shop that repaired locomotives. During

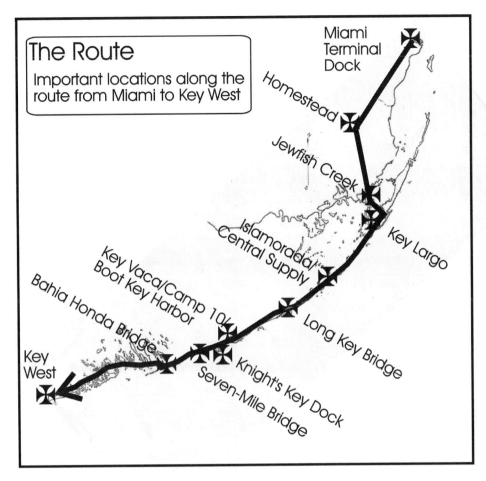

The Route

Important locations along the route from Miami to Key West

Miami Terminal Dock

Homestead

Jewfish Creek

Key Largo

Islamorada/Central Supply

Key Vaca/Camp 10/Boot Key Harbor

Long Key Bridge

Bahia Honda Bridge

Key West

Knight's Key Dock

Seven-Mile Bridge

Fig. 5. The overall route to Key West.

Fig. 6. Miami Terminal Docks—early headquarters for the project. (Monroe County Public Library)

the early construction period, this locomotive maintenance work was shifted to St. Augustine, and the Miami facility was retooled to build special equipment for the Extension project, including cement mixers, houseboats, and wooden forms for the concrete arches for the Extension bridges. At least five large quarterboats and as many as seven steam-powered cement mixing barges and derricks were built at these facilities. Other equipment, such as pile drivers, specialized barges and lighters, and even some of the drawbridge fabrications, were assembled at the Terminal Docks.

The site also became a shipyard, keeping the large fleet of Extension steamers in repair. In the early days of the Extension work, all of the supplies bound for the Keys left from the Terminal Docks. By mid-April 1908, boat repair facilities and machine shops were complete and operational at Boot Key, and the Terminal Docks facilities were not needed for Extension work. The facility returned to its earlier role as a repair center for the F.E.C. locomotives.

Jewfish Creek

Jewfish Creek was a major route to Florida Bay from Miami on the "inside" (between the Keys and the mainland). It was possible to bring heavy equipment down Biscayne Bay to Jewfish Creek; thus this was a logical place to begin dredging and filling from the Keys up towards Homestead. Jewfish Creek became the first "target" as a downstream supply area. Workers put track down across the eighteen-mile stretch from Homestead towards Key Largo, reaching Jewfish Creek in December 1906. Here they built a swing bridge and a triangular-shaped dock so the steamers could be loaded from trains at Jewfish Creek instead of at the Miami Terminal Docks.

This reduced the number of supply lines considerably, but there was still some steamer supply traffic between Miami and the Keys.

Central Supply (Islamorada)

The Extension plan included building a major supply depot in the Matecumbe Keys. This was located a few miles above the Long Key Bridge, under construction from 1906 through 1907. Central Supply sported a dock that could handle steamer and barge traffic. Steel rails reached Central Supply in early May 1907; it was fully operational by mid-May.

Key Vaca/Camp 10/Boot Key Harbor

Halfway between Key Largo and Key West lay the large island of Key Vaca. About two miles from the western end of the key, Camp No. 10 was established in 1905. This was first a site for low-level grading operations, but later Camp No. 10 became the center for a large-scale terminal. Workers built a great dock and turnaround track, as well as the infrastructure for a town that was to last for a few years after the railway was completed. This town became known as Marathon. Two miles to the east of Camp No. 10 lay the Boot Key Harbor complex. With two huge marine railways, a number of houses, and a large machine shop, Boot Key Harbor had replaced the functions of the Miami Terminal Docks by 1908.

Knight's Key Dock

The Knight's Key Dock was the penultimate rail/steamer station before the final terminal at Key West was completed. Construction began in January 1906, and work continued on this project until it was completed in 1908. It began as a freestanding platform nearly a mile offshore of

Fig. 7. Dock in Marathon on Florida Bay at Camp No. 10. (Wright Langley Archives)

Fig. 8. Knight's Key Dock grows as a platform offshore from Knight's Key. Pigeon Key is in the distance. Knight's Key is to the far right, not visible in this picture. (Museums at Crane Point Hammock)

Fig. 9. Completed terminal dock in Key West. (Al Perez)

Knight's Key and was in service as a materials transfer point long before it was finally connected to the mainland by a railroad trestle. By June 15, 1906, the dock was 115 feet long; in July it was accepting loads of crushed rock for redistribution to other sites in the Keys. At this time, service at the dock had grown enough to require a customs collector, a sub-agent from the Key West customs office.

There was no rail service to Knight's Key Dock at this time. In April 1906, workers began a dock from Knight's Key that eventually connected to the Knight's Key Dock. This was a temporary, light-use dock that was later replaced with a sturdy trestle for commercial service. The first piles for the Knight's Key Dock trestle were set in October 1907. The trestle was completed and final rail laid on the day it opened, January 22, 1908.

Key West

One of the three natural harbors in Florida, Key West was the ultimate destination of the Extension project. In terms of logistics, it was a far run from Miami for the supply steamers. During the course of the construction project, Key West grew by four hundred acres under the direction of Howard Trumbo. Much of this land was for the growing terminal, but some was also needed for storing materials brought in by steamers. Initially cement for the Long Key and Knight's Key Bridges was stored in Key West. Later the cement shipments went directly to Knight's Key Dock, where they were redistributed as needed from Marathon and Pigeon Key.

Priorities

The Key West Extension was a triumph of good planning and logistics. The project planners, always wary of timelines and length of supply lines, moved the Extension program in a logical way to accomplish their goal with minimal expenditures. A key to accomplishing this was establishing a major center in the middle of the Florida Keys. This center, in the general area of what is now the western end of Key Vaca and Knight's Key, gave birth to the town of Marathon. It is a common misconception that the Key West Extension began at Miami, pushed down to Homestead, then leaped to Key Largo, coursed over the middle Keys, and finished in Key West in some kind of linear fashion. In fact, the entire project was under construction from late 1905 through 1912 in a parallel fashion, with activity under way all along the Keys. In some areas, workers at primitive camps did nothing more than scrabble fill together for months at a time. This fill lay baking in the sun for a year or more before track-laying crews arrived to add ties and rails. Some camps flourished for a few months, then were abandoned, later to be reopened when needed for additional projects. The activities of the overall construction project were carefully choreographed in all areas of the Keys. The final span was set on January 21, 1912, a half-mile west of Marathon–it was planned that way from the beginning. Marathon was the key element of the grand scheme.

An editorial from the *Key West Citizen* (a newspaper owned by Flagler) in October 1907 recognized the considerable advance thinking that the construction engineers put into the project. The editorial was a response to rumors published by the *Miami Herald* that the project was about to be ended. To quote the *Citizen:*

The plans for this road are not made as the work progresses, neither is the material ordered just as it was needed. For years experts have been busy on the plans for this gigantic engineering feat. Every inch of the right of way has been carefully examined, every obstacle noted and provided for, and before the first shovel of dirt was thrown, the engineers knew to the ounce how much steel and cement would be needed. Orders were placed far in advance timed for delivery as fast as it could be used.

The plan was strong, the plan was good, and, with a few exceptions, the plan was not changed from 1904 to the completion of the project.

If the Extension engineers assembled a "think tank" operation to prioritize their project (and we must suppose that they did), they may very well have chalked a list of tasks on their blackboard. Choreographing these tasks was the prime responsibility of James Meredith. Here is how his list may have looked (with commentary).

1. *Build tools.* Assemble the tools to build the railway, mostly vessels for transportation and construction. This would be the first and greatest railroad project to be built largely by floating machines. Many of these vessels would move materials; others would be highly specialized to mix cement, drive pilings, dredge, and do other work from the water. Almost all of these special tools would have to be built by the F.E.C. because they were not otherwise available.

2. *Minimize water transport routes.* Keep over-water supply routes as short as possible. Transportation by stern-wheel steamer was slow and expensive. Transportation by rail was relatively inexpensive, and it was important to get track down from Miami to lower distribution points as quickly as possible.

3. *Complete infrastructure tasks early.* Accomplish the groundwork as soon as possible. Grade all of the high land for the right-of-way early so that when it became possible to lay track, this labor-intensive task would be completed.

4. *Establish temporary terminals.* Establish temporary terminals along the way as soon as possible so vessels could bring in supplies and laborers by train instead of by boat. The main temporary terminals were at Jewfish Creek, then Central Supply near Islamorada, and finally a temporary terminal at Knight's Key Dock. This terminal let the F.E.C. begin international shipping four years before the project was completed and also provided a central point for shipping materials.

Fig.10. Complete infrastructure tasks. This involved bringing the Keys up to grade. This photo was taken at the north end of Tavernier Creek in November 1905. (Museums at Crane Point Hammock)

5. *Establish local command centers.* Put the center of command in
    the center of the action. Move the construction headquarters
    from Miami down to the Keys as soon as infrastructure was in
    place to do so. Communications would be speedier, and impor-
    tant engineers would be on the spot for quick decisions.

6. *Get to Knight's Key!* Put down track for the run to Knight's Key at
    any cost and by any method. While there were a number of con-
    crete bridges required between Miami and Knight's Key, there
    were also areas that were suitable for temporary trestles, such as
    the gaps between upper and lower Matecumbe, the Tom's Harbor
    Keys, and other crossings over shallow water. Workers built
    wooden trestles on pilings that were later replaced with concrete
    arch bridges after the railway reached Knight's Key in 1908.

7. *Minimize bridges.* Contain costs by minimizing the number of
    bridges that had to be built. It was much cheaper to fill in
    between Keys and build up roadways across mangrove and shal-
    low water areas with rock and marl than it was to build concrete

Fig. 11. The General Office (main construction headquarters) was established in Marathon in 1908. (Monroe County Public Library)

or steel bridges. Indeed, many of the Keys were connected with fill. This became a problem later in the project, however, after the engineers learned that hurricane surges easily washed out the fill. They then changed this element of the plan and increased the number of bridges.

8. *Use local materials.* Use materials found in the Keys as close to the construction site as possible. This minimizes moving earth and rock from remote locations at great expense and effort. As the project progressed, engineers found ways to use local materials to save the company money.

9. *Be flexible!* The engineers knew that the survey and original plan were subject to changes during the course of construction. For example, they could not predict hurricanes and their effects, so they changed their plans based on what they learned from these storms. They also changed their plans dramatically by building each of the major bridges in a different fashion than initially planned.

With these priorities in mind, the steps of the plan became clear. Under Meredith, the F.E.C. Construction Division began assembling a fleet as early as 1904. Meredith directed crews to begin the low-level infrastructure work throughout the Keys, with rough camps at many sites engaged in clearing and grading operations. To shorten expensive steamer supply lines, several areas were selected to become "nodes," sites where temporary terminals were built to serve as distribution points for further operations. The first was at Jewfish Creek, the second at Islamorada (Central Supply), and finally a major node was built at Key Vaca and the Knight's Key Dock. Once trains and ships were running from Knight's Key Terminal, with a major distribution center in Marathon and a repair center at Boot Key, the project became much easier.

The accompanying maps show the overall progress of the Extension project through the construction years. While the growing rail line jumps from node to node, it is important to note that several of the final bridges were not completed until years after the track passed over some waterways. Temporary wooden bridges crossed several channels; these were replaced with concrete viaducts later. In some areas, the track was laid on temporary fill. This fill was increased and hardened after hurricanes washed out the initial track. Though the project appeared to be progressing in a straight line, there were a number of places where the rule was, "Get the trains to Knight's Key any way you can today—we'll build it better tomorrow."

The Team

Flagler and Parrott assembled an engineering team to plan the best way to go about the project. Construction Engineer J. C. Meredith was also head of the Administration Department. Meredith was a specialist in reinforced concrete and had recently completed a dock in Tampico, Mexico, before he signed on with the Flagler team in July 1904. Meredith was described as ". . . a man of highly sensitive perception, and . . . quick to grasp a situation, carrying every detail great and small

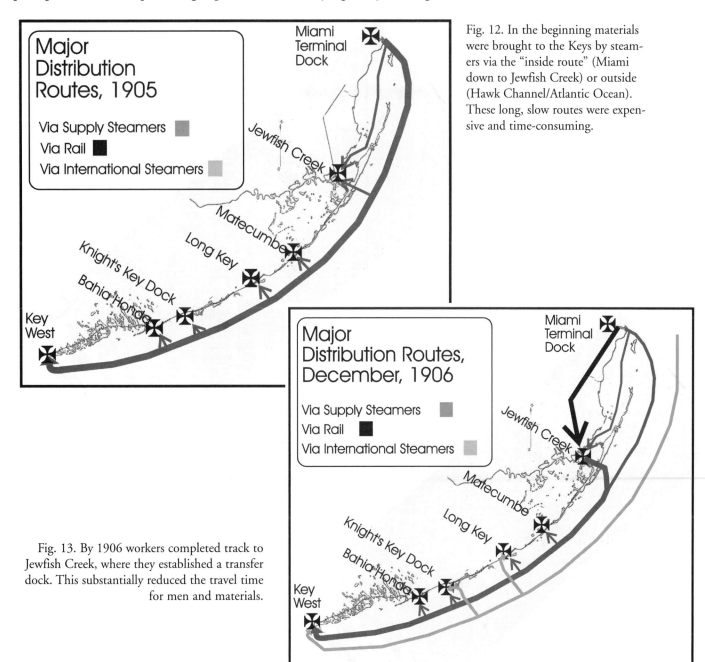

Fig. 12. In the beginning materials were brought to the Keys by steamers via the "inside route" (Miami down to Jewfish Creek) or outside (Hawk Channel/Atlantic Ocean). These long, slow routes were expensive and time-consuming.

Fig. 13. By 1906 workers completed track to Jewfish Creek, where they established a transfer dock. This substantially reduced the travel time for men and materials.

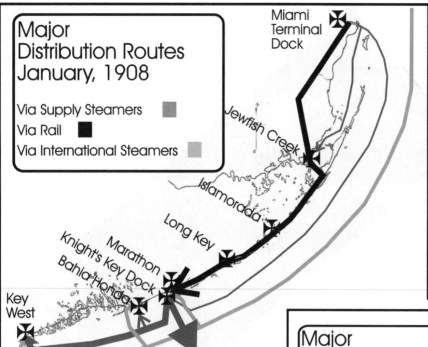

Fig. 14. Once the major docks at Marathon were finished in January 1908, trains moved most of the materials and supplies to this area. The project was only 50 miles from Key West at this time.

Fig. 15. The track was completed in January 1912. A large part of the transportation fleet was taken off line and trains did most of the heavy hauling after this.

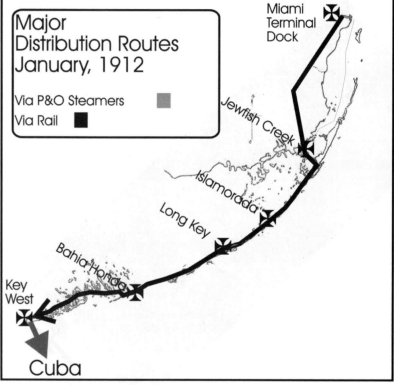

in his mind, and going about his affairs in a leisurely, methodical way that brings the best and quickest results."

Under Meredith were departments for Design, Plant Construction, Accounting, and Transportation. Meredith's staff in Miami was not large; only fifteen employees were listed in July 1906. Marine Stephens, Meredith's stenographer,

had the distinction of being the only woman employed in the vast enterprise.

The Department of Design was in charge of planning all of the bridges, viaducts, docks, and special equipment needed for the project. R. W. Carter, head of this department, had six staff employees working for him. The Department of Design produced the blueprints and specifications for the cement mixers, excavators, and all of the specialized watercraft built at the Terminal Docks. This small department worked very closely with the Plant Construction Department.

The largest department at the Miami end of the project, Plant Construction, listed sixteen hundred employees on its staff, including sixty engineers and superintendents. The Plant Construction Department built and expanded the Terminal Docks continuously from 1905 through 1907, building a number of quarterboats, cement mixers, excavators, and forms for the concrete piers and arches. The department also built many small boats, fabricated steel drawspans, operated a major machine shop, and repaired all of the watercraft used by the Extension. Of all the departments, Plant Construction was the most active in the field and moved its offices closer to the action in Marathon by 1908. William J. Krome was the principal assistant engineer in charge of the Plant Construction Department at the Terminal Docks and later in Marathon. Krome later became the construction engineer in charge of the project when Meredith died in 1908.

Fig. 16. Mr. James C. Meredith, construction engineer in charge of the Extension project until his death in 1908. (Monroe County Public Library)

The Accounting Department also began its work in the Terminal Docks office in Miami and later moved part of its operation to Marathon. Head of the department was W. J. Russell, who had purview of all materials and payroll accounts for the labor force. Accounting was a small department, listing twenty people on its staff in

Fig. 17. Excavator on barge working with clamshell bucket. (Historical Museum of Southern Florida)

July 1906. Carlton Corliss, a junior member of the department at this time, later moved to Marathon and became a central figure in the town.

The department concerned with logistics belonged to E. F. Rue, head of the Transportation Department. In 1906 Rue had forty staff members, including the captains who ran the steamers that distributed materials from Miami to the Keys. Rue spent a week or more each month down in the Keys, and his department grew, then shrank, as the Extension proceeded in the last years of construction. The Transportation Department was responsible for getting all of the building materials, construction workers, and crucial supplies—water and food—to the camps. In 1906 the Extension operation listed three tugs, eight stern-wheel steamers, twenty-seven gasoline launches, fourteen houseboats, eight work boats with derricks and cement mixers, three pile drivers, one floating machine shop, and seventy-two barges.

Meredith and his team were "bright young men on their way up." They were not new at construction or construction management, and all had demonstrated proficiency at their tasks. They looked forward to tackling the Extension project. They expected several years of employment from the work and great kudos at the end for a grand task brought to a successful conclusion. They embraced the plan and put it to work.

Fig. 18. William Krome became engineer in charge of the project. (Monroe County Public Library)

Fig. 19. Accounting office in Marathon. (Monroe County Public Library)

2

Reshaping the Keys

MUCH OF THIS STORY is about moving earth and rock from one location to another. Excavators, dredges, mules, and the strong backs of many men shifted the shorelines of the Keys dramatically from 1905 to 1916. By the time the roadbed was completed, they had built nearly twenty-two miles of filled causeway and eighteen miles of bridges between the Keys. Henry M. Flagler called his project "landscape gardening." The ambitious project is even more awesome when you consider the primitive machines engineers designed and workers built to do the job. Most of these machines were powered by steam engines, but the engineers experimented with gasoline engines for some of their tools.

The F.E.C. kept detailed records of all of the rock, marl, sand, riprap, and ballast moved throughout the Keys. Each resident engineer filed a weekly report from each construction section describing the number of cubic yards of each type of fill as it was collected and moved to other sites. From these reports we are able to know how much earth was moved, when it was

moved, and where it went. The total amount of material moved for the Extension project was recorded as 17,940,837 cubic yards. In today's terms, this is the equivalent of more than one million dump trucks! If all of this material were molded into a solid cube, it would be 785 feet wide, long, and tall. By comparison, the Washington Monument is 550 feet tall.

Dredges did much of the work, moving sand to build up the grade and marl to make a protective covering on the walls of the roadbeds and causeways. Excavators, both floating and land-based, scooped up chunks of rock and riprap at the roadbed site and in quarries. Together these tools moved 16.78 million cubic yards. The amount moved by hand for manual grading—a mere 1.16 million cubic yards— seems minuscule at only 6.47 percent of the earth moved, but in human terms this totaled a lot of tired backs and aching muscles.

The original roadbed was modified dramatically from the rudimentary line that coursed into Key West in 1912. In the years from 1912 to

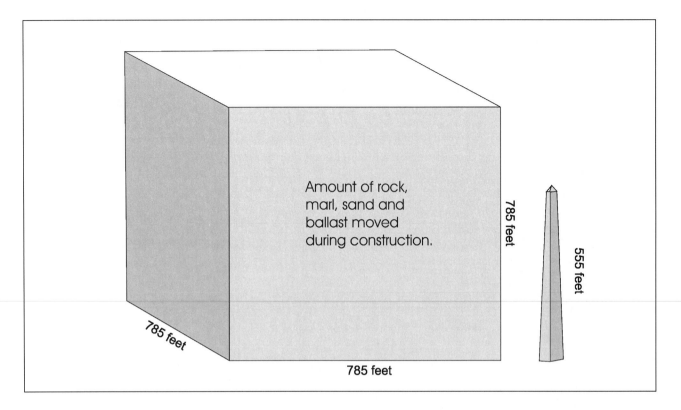

1916, the right-of-way was widened and the roadbed elevated to safer heights and with better materials. At sites where concrete arch bridges replaced the original wooden trestles, workers imported much fill to bring the grade to the viaduct level.

At many sites along the roadway, there were not enough local materials of the right quality to build up the grade to the desired height. Thus the rock or sand or marl had to be quarried at one location and transported to where it was needed. Engineers found numerous sites for rock fill along the right-of-way and established quarries at Rockdale, Key Largo, Windley's Island, and Teakettle Rock Pit. Two quarries at Windley's Island produced most of the rock, and a station appropriately named Quarry was eventually established there. Some of the original quarries are still visible and open to visitors at the Windley Key Fossil Reef State Geological Site.

Total materials placed on the right-of-way

Numbers are in cubic yards	From Dredges and Excavators	By Manual Grading
1905-06	428,901	0
1906-07	2,037,818	0
1907-08	1,017,060	0
1908-09*	1,021,484	852,149
1909-10	593,946	132,250
1910-11	1,205,797	32,723
1911-12	1,773,738	138,931
1912-13	2,707,850	4,805
1913-14*	3,131,982	0
1914-15	1,298,700	0
1915-16	1,562,703	0
	16,779,979	**1,160,858**
	Total materials	17,940,837

Fig. 20. Amounts of material moved by machines vs. human labor. The asterisk for 1908-09 notes that 1905-1908 data was combined in the 1908 Annual Report. The asterisk for 1913-14 indicates an underestimate; one page was missing from the Annual Report.

Fig. 21. Moving rock, sand, marl and earth—this was the story of the Extension roadbed—landscape gardening on a grand scale. This photograph is from Camp No. 8 on Windley's Island. (Museums at Crane Point Hammock)

Fig. 22. Shows how much material was moved in each year of the construction project by dredges, from quarries, and by manual grading. It is interesting to note that by the time the railroad was in operation to Key West in 1912, only 40.8 percent—less than half of the materials—had been placed. The remaining 59.2 percent of the earth moved was done after the line was operating. This indicates that the Extension, while operating, was extremely rudimentary in 1912, and that the engineers knew that they had to finish the job to make a safe, high, hard roadbed for a permanent line.

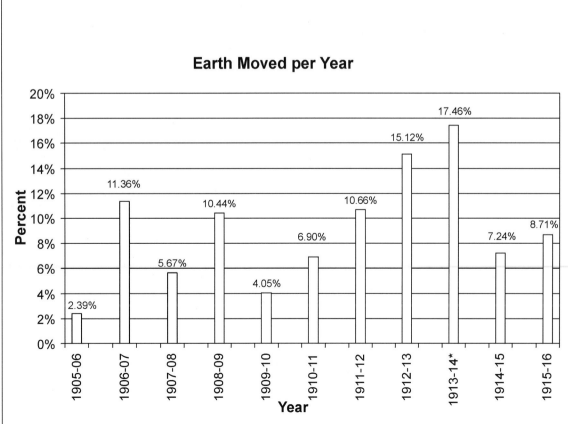

Earth Moved per Year

Fig. 23. Mature grade level, location unknown. This photo shows the original track level to the right and the completed elevated fill in the center. The machine appears to be an excavator modified to operate on land and assist in laying new track and spreading ballast. (Steele)

THE EXCAVATOR

The excavator was a digging machine designed by the F.E.C. Construction Division to move materials on land or water. The digging tool was a clamshell bucket raised and lowered from the end of a long boom. The boom, mounted on the front of the excavator and controlled by two cables, could be swung from side to side. These cables were reeled in or released by hoisting drums turned by a thirty-horsepower Otto gasoline engine inside the excavator. The boom swung to the side with the bucket in the "open" position, then dropped the bucket onto the targeted ground. The captain then used the haulback cable to close the bucket, raise it, and swing it to the middle of the roadbed dump area.

When excavators were used on barges, they were simply towed into position and anchored. They changed their position by changing the length of their mooring lines or moving the anchors. These floating excavators were very useful, but on land they were ungainly and difficult to move. The land-based machines had four double-flanged wheels on each side mounted to two twelve-by-twelve-foot wooden timbers. They rode on temporary track that was moved forward as necessary. They were heavy, clumsy, needed constant repairs, and tended to slip off the track frequently. It took so much time and effort to keep these machines running and to move them that they did not spend a lot of time digging. One engineer kept accurate records of the amount of sand that could be moved with an excavator compared to the amount that could be moved with men. He concluded that it was faster and more economical to use laborers. This same engineer, Howard Egleston, observed that Henry Flagler wished to employ as many people as possible for the Extension project, so Egleston generally avoided using laborsaving equipment.

Fig. 24. Excavator on lower Matecumbe Key building its own roadbed. (Museums at Crane Point Hammock)

Output from Quarries, Marl Pits and Sand Pits

Station	Rockdale Quarry 20,038	Key Largo Quarry 21,987	Windley's Island Q. 23,135	Central Sp. Marl Pit 23,432	Midway Sand Pit 23,633	Long Key Sand Pit 24,063	Crawl Key Sand Pit 24,610	Key Vaca Marl Pit 25,021	Teakettle Rock Pit 25,494
1905-06									
1906-07	16,060	18,840							
1907-08	171	18,840	57,463		84,446				
1908-09			78,385		128,605				
1909-10				144,210		32,850			
1910-11				499,770	8,020	39,558	180,720		
1911-12				792,120		300			
1912-13			2,068	126,710				36,750	
1913-14			564					936,180	
1914-15			48	324,550				470,460	600
1915-16				363,600				291,420	
Total	16,231	37,680	138,528	2,250,960	221,071	72,708	180,720	1,734,810	600

Output from Quarries, Marl Pits and Sand Pits   (continued)

Station	B. Honda Sand Pit 25,582	Spanish H. Marl Pit 25,806	Pine Ch. Marl Pit 26,076	Bow Ch. Marl Pit 26,539	Shark Key Marl Pit 27,017	Boca Ch. Marl Pit 27,320	Key West Slip Rock 27,870	Total Output per Year
1905-06								0
1906-07								34,900
1907-08								160,920
1908-09	17,543	1,628						226,161
1909-10								177,060
1910-11	80,426					298,470	7,194	1,114,158
1911-12			238,320		506,800	120,990		1,658,530
1912-13		251,970	506,020	786,840	644,770	192,810	126,211	2,674,149
1913-14		645,530			561,700			2,143,974
1914-15		35,430		360	106,560			938,008
1915-16		692,010			43,320		107,190	1,497,540
Total	97,969	1,626,568	744,340	787,200	1,863,150	612,270	240,595	10,625,400

Total material moved from quarries   10,625,400
Total material moved in entire construction project   17,940,837

Percent moved from quarries   59.22%

Fig. 25. Total output from the quarries, including rock, ballast, sand, and marl. The totals show that about 60 percent of the material that was moved was transported some distance from its origin. The other 40 percent of material was pumped in from the sea bottom or blasted from the right of way and placed locally.

Fig. 26. Excavator filling Goodwin car with marl at an unidentified marl pit. (Historical Museum of South Florida)

The first generation of the Extension was the most difficult to build since there were no train tracks in place. But once this rudimentary Extension was in place, it was much easier to move additional materials to build up the roadbed. Rock, marl, and ballast were no longer transported by wheelbarrows or mule carts but by railway cars. Workers used a special piece of rolling stock, the Goodwin car, to carry material from quarries and marl pits to construction sites. These cars held a lot of material and were designed to dump their loads by tilting to one side or the other.

Early in the project in the upper Keys, workers built the roadbed to grade level with sand, then buttressed it on the sides with coral rock. The sand was brought in by hand or pumped in from offshore excavators. After the hurricane of 1906, the engineers determined that this was not the best way to build a roadbed or causeway: storm surges moved the rock and the sand escaped. They then experimented with the local marl as a roadbed agent. Marl, a highly calcareous base of sediments found in local areas near

the Keys, was a "sticky" composition of marine shell fragments and remains of marine calcareous alga. The marl hardened in a few weeks to a rocklike composition of limestone. Marl turned out to be the material of choice for "hardening" roadbeds. Surveyors sought sources for this wonder material and found several marl pits in the nearby Keys' waters. The following list contains these sites and their outputs in cubic yards:

Central Supply Marl Pit	2,250,960
Shark Key Marl Pits	1,863,150
Key Vaca Marl Pit	1,734,810
Spanish Harbor Marl Pit	1,626,568
Bow Channel Marl Pit	787,200
Pine Channel Marl Pit	744,340
Boca Chica Marl Pit	612,270

In most cases these marl pits were located at some distance from the main line. However, because marl was a valuable material, laborers built trestles from the main line to the marl pit areas. They stationed excavators at the marl pits—sometimes for more than a year at a

Fig. 27. The Boot Key Harbor marl trestles extended south and west from the area near the train station in Marathon. This photo shows them under construction. There are remains of these trestles today overgrown by mangroves. (Brian Schmitt)

time—and continually ran Goodwin cars back and forth from the marl pit areas to the construction dump sites. In Boot Key Harbor, for example, engineers designed a trestle that began at the Marathon Station and coursed 1,370 feet southward into the harbor to the Key Vaca Marl Pit. After a couple of years, when laborers had depleted the marl near the trestle, a second trestle nearly a mile long was built in Boot Key Harbor. These two pits produced nearly ten percent of the fill for the entire construction project. The site where these trestles entered Boot Key Harbor shows the pits' remains today.

The shallow waters to the south of Shark Key covered a rich mine of marl, and the engineers established a camp on the fill that passed by Shark Key. Workers built a trestle 5,400 feet south of the main line to get to this pit. Opened in August 1911, in the first year it produced 506,800 cubic yards of marl, which was distrib-

uted from the Saddle Bunch Keys to Key West. In the following year, workers built another trestle in the same area. Shark Key Trestle 2 was initially 3,930 feet long, then lengthened by 870 feet in 1914. In 1914 a third trestle was built at the Shark Key Marl Pits and Trestle 1 was closed. During the four years that the Shark Key Marl Pits operated, the three pits produced 1,863,150 cubic yards of fill, more than ten percent of the total earth moved for the Extension project. Modern nautical charts warn boaters of "submerged pilings" in the Similar Sound area. These are the remnants of the trestles that led to the marl pits.

In many respects, the Extension was never finished. Workers kept adding material to the roadbed long after 1916. When they needed more marl in 1918, they opened a seventh marl pit in the Kemp Channel area. Here, as in previous years, they built a trestle and dredged fill

Fig. 28. Work train hauling eight Goodwin cars from a marl pit. This appears to be at Boot Key Harbor. Workers built a number of trestles to locations far from the main line to mine this special material. The excavator is in the distance. (Historical Museum of South Florida)

from both sides of the trestle as needed. Figures 30 through 35 tell the story of this trestle.

Today as you drive through the middle and lower Keys, you may stop almost anywhere along the old roadbed and see the remaining marl fill. Generally gray and lumpy and laced with bits of shell fragments, the material is slippery when wet but tends to stay in place. At the south end of the Bahia Honda Bridge, you can see acres of the original marl exposed. Over the years, storms have taken their toll on this fill, but it is still substantially in place.

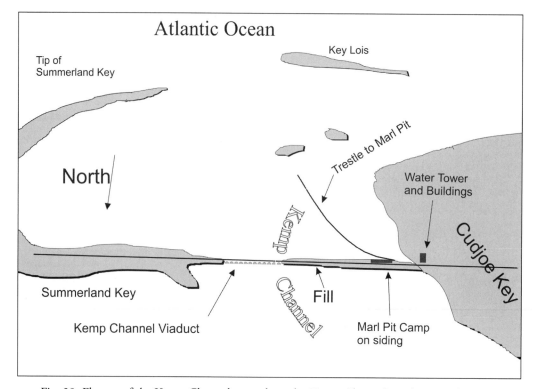

Fig. 29. Flyover of the Kemp Channel area where the Kemp Channel Marl Pit was located.

Fig. 30. An excavator at work building the trestle for the Kemp Channel Marl Pit. (Louis "Pete" Bow)

Fig. 31. Trestle extends more than a mile south of the main line. The remains of the trestle are labeled as "submerged pilings" on nautical charts. The dredged area is noticeable in aerial photographs today. (Louis "Pete" Bow)

Fig. 32. Dredge Babcock placing fill behind retaining wall at the Kemp Channel Marl Pit campsite. (Louis "Pete" Bow)

Fig. 33. The Kemp Channel Marl Pit camp on the side of the causeway. The two train cars in the foreground are on a siding. The main line runs between these cars and the three buildings on the bay side of the track. The landmass at the top left is the east side of Cudjoe Key. (Louis "Pete" Bow)

Fig. 34. Buildings at the Kemp Channel Marl Pit Camp. The camp grew as the pit was developed. (Louis "Pete" Bow)

Fig. 35. View to the west of the siding, trestle, and camp at Kemp Channel Marl Pit. The water tower is on Cudjoe Key. The camp is well developed with a complete retaining wall. Traces of this wall and some of the trestle pilings are still in place. (Louis "Pete" Bow)

Fig. 36. Same location as above in 1934. The photographer is atop the water tower shooting to the east at the causeway and Kemp Channel Viaduct. The Kemp Channel Marl Pit camp at the siding is gone, but there are still traces of the marl pit trestle visible curving toward the right. Photo from author's collection.

3
Vessels of the F.E.C.

THE PLAN FOR THE KEY WEST EXTENSION first took its shape from the logistics of moving the great quantities of materials to the Keys. It may seem strange that a railroad would begin with ships and boats, but since the project was largely over water, the first step was to secure vessels suitable for transportation and construction. E. F. Rue, transportation chief, began acquiring vessels early in 1905, including quarterboats for housing and steamers to move materials and supplies from Miami to the Keys. Because the Extension was built in shallow waters, the vessels needed to be able to run in a puddle. Rue commissioned Southern Shipbuilding in Jacksonville for 28 barges; he purchased others as they could be found, and many were built at the Terminal Docks in Miami. In 1906 and 1907, the F.E.C. also built many specialized barges to mix cement, to dredge and fill, and to house workers for the project.

The F.E.C. listed several categories of working vessels, including steamers, launches, tugs, barges and specialized barges (cement mixers, pile drivers, and the like). The barges and spe-

Fig. 37. Steamer *Columbia* pushing a barge and a pile driver. (Historical Museum of South Florida)

cialized equipment had no motive power and were towed or pushed from place to place by tugs and steamers. Launches were small vessels with propellers and gasoline engines; these were used for survey work, transporting supervisory staff to remote locations, transporting workers, and general purpose hauling. The most interesting vessels used in the Keys were the steamers, steam-powered paddlewheel ships acquired by Rue from the Mississippi River area.

The Steamers

All of the paddlewheel fleet were stern-wheelers, veterans of the Mississippi and other shallow-water rivers. The F.E.C. purchased most of them, but some were hired or leased as necessary. The core fleet included *Phil Scheckel, Virginia, Kennedy, Peerless, St. Lucie,*

Fig. 38. Steamer *Peerless* with water tanks on barge. (Museums at Crane Point Hammock)

Fig. 39. Stern wheel steamer *Wanderer.* These vessels, fresh from service on the Mississippi River, look entirely too grand and festive to serve as workboats. In truth, they were the "pick-up trucks" of the Extension construction project, pushing and towing barges and carrying materials and supplies in their ample lower deck. (Todd Tinkham)

Fig. 40. Steamer *Phil Scheckel*. This vessel appears less grand than some of the others. (Curtis Skomp)

Wanderer, Biscayne, Reindeer, and *Columbia.* The first four vessels were acquired in 1905. Relatively small, they ranged in size from 97 feet (*Peerless*) to 122 feet (*Kennedy*). *Virginia* was an older vessel, built in 1893; the others were only a few years old when construction commenced. They were towed down from Mobile by the tug *Sybil,* another early acquisition.

The steamers worked long and hard during the early construction years but began to run out of work once the Knight's Key dock was connected to Miami. They served as supply boats and also as push boats for barges. By September 1907, several boats were laid up in the Miami River. Sturdy *Phil Scheckel* was temporarily retired at this time; the only remaining steamers were the *Virginia, Peerless, St. Lucie,* and *Columbia,* all of which worked in the lower Keys

during the last four years of construction.

Steamer *Phil Scheckel* is well described in specification sheets from F.E.C. records. The vessel was 111.5 feet long, 24.8 feet wide, and drew 4.2 feet of water. She had two boilers and two horizontal keel-condensing engines that turned a paddlewheel 13 feet in diameter and 14.5 feet wide. The wooden paddlewheel had 12 buckets. The smokestack was 20 inches in diameter and 24 feet high. The vessel was complete with a generator, ample electric service (120 volt), and numerous pumps. There were accommodations for two pilots, two quartermasters, four deck hands, two engineers, three firemen, and a steward.

Phil Scheckel and all of the steamers were serviced (often) at the Miami Terminal Docks. This facility, initially a locomotive repair shop,

Fig. 41. *St. Lucie* played host to guests on excursions, and was very well maintained. (Museums at Crane Point Hammock)

was well equipped to deal with steam engines, and there are numerous reports of the steamers having a complete overhaul at the Terminal Docks, including the replacement of boilers and engines. By 1908 this repair work was carried out at the Boot Key Machine Shop in Marathon, and for the most part the steamers did not have to return to Miami after the Boot Key shop opened.

Most of the steamers ran aground or suffered minor mishaps during their years of service, but the *St. Lucie* had the worst luck. On October 17, 1906, she sank off Elliot's Key during a hurricane. In November she was declared to be scrap and valued at $50. Nevertheless, the F.E.C. raised the derelict (*St. Lucie* was a steel-hulled vessel), brought it to the Terminal Docks, and then rebuilt the vessel at an expense that exceeded her replacement cost. It took the carpenters and mechanics in Miami more than six months to rebuild *St. Lucie;* in July 1907, she was back in service. Her task at this time was to run supplies from Central Supply in upper

Matecumbe down to the lower Keys. In April 1908, she was laid up in Boot Key Harbor with little work because the railway was now completed to Marathon. She served the ongoing work in the lower Keys, but in May 1909, the *St. Lucie* was towed to Boot Key Harbor after hitting a rock at Bahia Honda. She sank in 12 feet of water but was easily raised and repaired. Three months later in August, *St. Lucie* blew a cylinder head at Jewfish Creek, damaging internal machinery. Engineer Alex McDonald was blown off the ship by the escaping steam, landed in the mangroves, and was seriously hurt. *St. Lucie* was towed to the Terminal Docks in Miami. She was repaired and was back in service by October. In Boot Key Harbor at the time of the October 9, 1909, hurricane, *St. Lucie* was the lucky vessel for the first time—she and *Kennedy* were undamaged by the hurricane; most of the other vessels at Boot Key were sunk by the storm. *St. Lucie's* captain, Ed Graham, was commended for his good seamanship during the storm; he saved

Fig. 42. Sad photo/post-card of *St. Lucie* after being salvaged in 1906. This hull was rebuilt to her former splendor by the carpenters at the Miami Terminal Docks. (Monroe County Public Library)

Fig. 43. Steamer *Virginia*. Note the great amount of space for materials inside on the lower deck. Also note how low the vessel is to the water—steamers were vulnerable to rough seas. (Museums at Crane Point Hammock)

the crew of the *Peerless*, which overturned in Boot Key Harbor.

The stern-wheel steamers were designed for river navigation and were marginally suited for work in the Keys. They had very little freeboard, and in heavy weather, were prone to taking water over the side. Waters inside the Keys in Florida Bay were seldom rough enough to bother the steamers. The waters in Hawk Channel inside the reef line were also calmer than offshore ocean waters and were manageable for the steamers under most conditions. However, it did not take

Fig. 44. Officers on *St. Lucie* at dinner. (Museums at Crane Point Hammock)

Fig. 45. P&O Steamer *Montauk* at Knight's Key Dock. (Monroe County Public Library)

much of a storm to swamp the low vessels, and this happened more than once during the construction period.

The steamers were well maintained in spite of being considered workboats. A steward served the officers' meals, and proper shipboard discipline was observed at all times, even though the vessels were engaged in inelegant activities.

There were other steamers involved in the master plan. The Peninsular and Occidental Steamship Line (P&O), established in 1899 by the F.E.C., began with three screw-propulsion steamers acquired to carry passengers to the Keys and beyond. These vessels were in service to Key West, and by 1908 to Knight's Key, transporting passengers to Cuba and Key West. Because of their sixteen-foot draft they needed deep-water ports or long docks like the one on Knight's Key from land out to deep water.

Steamer *Montauk* was one of these early P&O acquisitions, purchased by the F.E.C. in 1899. This vessel initially ran from Miami to

Havana and Key West until the track was completed to Knight's Key Dock in 1908. Then *Montauk* began regular service from Knight's Key Dock to Key West and Havana, never going to Miami again except for emergency runs after the hurricane of 1909, when service was disrupted for a month.

The F.E.C. chartered three oceangoing steamers for four years to transport cement from Germany to the construction site in the Keys. These steamers, *Nubia, Savilla,* and *Alexandria* were large—the *Alexandria* was 450 feet long. Their initial run was to Key West, but after Knight's Key Dock was completed, they brought materials into the middle Keys and Pigeon Key for distribution down the line. Outside of Key West, the steamers anchored offshore, where they transferred cement barrels to lighters to be ferried ashore or to waiting cement mixers.

Quarterboats

In the early part of the Extension campaign, quarterboats were considered the best form of housing for the workers. These boats were large floating dormitories. When workers completed a job at a given location, they moved on to another site—

and their home moved with them. Quarter-boats were relatively inexpensive to build, and the Miami Terminal Docks facilities cranked out a number of them. Records show that the Docks began two houseboats in late April 1906, which were completed by August of that year. One of them was then sent to Knight's Key.

The standard F.E.C. houseboat was quite large. With a length of 60 feet, each held 160 workers. The upper deck was fitted out with furniture and bunks; the workers had a dining hall on the lower deck. The boats were weathertight and screened to keep out mosquitoes, flies, and other insects. These quarterboats were quite stable, and because they could be towed from site to site, were ideal for a railway construction project that was always on the move. With their shallow draft, they could be pulled right up to the shoreline and accessed by a short dock at many sites.

The F.E.C. initially planned to build 14 quarterboats for the project. At least five were completed. *Quarterboat 5* served as the main Extension office in Marathon, and was later used as offices for the subcontractor who put up the first steel deck plates for the Knight's Key

Fig. 46. Outside view of *Quarterboat No. 2* at Key Largo. The "bath house" unit hangs off the left end of the vessel. A water barge is fast alongside. This quarterboat is a sister ship of quarterboats 1 through 5. (Monroe County Public Library)

Fig. 47. Small quarterboat in canal at Marathon. Because of their shallow draft, these vessels could be brought right up to the shoreline. (Monroe County Public Library)

Fig. 48. Quarterboat housing the workers dredging the canals on each side of the 18-mile stretch from Key Largo to Jewfish Creek. (Museums at Crane Point Hammock)

Fig. 49. Inside *Quarterboat No. 2* at Knight's Key Dock. This section of the lower deck was a mess hall for the workers. (Museums at Crane Point Hammock)

Fig. 50. *Quarterboat No. 5* at Marathon. This boat was used for housing, then for office space, and was the center of the construction project for a few months until the General Office was completed nearby on the shore. (Monroe County Public Library)

Bridge. The hurricane of 1906, which ravaged the construction camp at Long Key, blew *Quarterboat 4* out to sea with many men on board. The boat was broken up offshore and 100 died. After this hurricane, the F.E.C. determined that houseboats were not safe enough in storms and their men were better off housed on land.

Quarterboats were gradually phased out, and more land-based camps were built with solid housing. Sites that were expected to be industrious for a year or more sported long bunkhouses such as those seen on Pigeon Key. The remaining quarterboats were still used in places, but were kept in very protected canals, such as Ohio Key.

A number of other houseboats were used by the F.E.C. that were not of the standard 160-bed design. Many of them had been purchased as hulls, then modified by construction carpenters. A few workers bought their own houseboats. C. S. Coe, resident engineer at Marathon and Pigeon Key, for example, purchased a small houseboat in Key West, then had it towed to the middle Keys. The boat served as his office, first in Marathon, then at Pigeon Key in 1907. For a time this houseboat was located onshore on Pigeon Key. His wife and three children lived on board for a large part of each year until 1911.

While the houseboat or quarterboat seemed at first to have promise as a portable living facility, the F.E.C. later discontinued their use for company purposes because of their great vulnerability to hurricanes. By 1909 houseboats were rarely used as company quarters except by private individuals or when moored in predredged "hurricane holes."

Tugboats

The F.E.C. owned several tugboats for general purpose hauling in the Keys. *Sybil*, on the job in 1906, was an early addition to the fleet, and towed several of the paddlewheel steamers to the Keys from Alabama. Other tugs included the *Pelton* (sunk at Knight's Key Dock in October 1909), *Dauntless, Hudson,* and *Sadie.*

Sybil was the largest tug, 85 feet long and 20 feet wide, and drew nearly 8 feet. Her 4-bladed propeller was 7 feet 2 inches in diameter. Powered by a compound condensing steam engine, she had several pumps, a generator system, and accommodations for two captains, two engineers, three firemen, four deck hands, and a steward. Her hull was wood, 3-inch pine planking on sides and deck with 4 by 8 inch pine frames on 18-inch centers. *Sybil* was built in 1905 and rebuilt in 1910 by the F.E.C. Tug *Sadie* was smaller (65 feet long) and drew only five feet of water. Because of her smaller size, she needed only a single captain, one engineer, one fireman, a deck hand, and a steward.

Fig. 51. Tug *Sybil*, one of the earliest F.E.C. acquisitions, worked hard for the Railway throughout the entire construction project. (Historical Museum of South Florida)

The tugs were frequently employed as towboats, hauling supplies and water down to the camps in the Keys. While their deep draft and propeller propulsion kept them offshore for the most part, they were able to get into some of the channels in the Keys and into Boot Key Harbor. Tugs were often called in to tow disabled steamers and other equipment to Miami or Boot Key for repairs. They were also used to move cement mixers and pile drivers into position for their work; these vessels had no propulsion of their own.

In the hurricane of 1909, *Sybil* was working at Bahia Honda; sister tug *Sadie* was in the same area near West Summerland Key. *Sybil* headed towards Bahia Honda as the storm approached. When the wind shifted to the northwest at 85 miles per hour, the *Sybil* was no longer in shelter, slipped her anchor, and was reportedly blown to pieces. Nine crew and the captain lost their lives; only one person survived. Washed ashore at Bahia Honda, he was found clinging to a railroad track with a wheelbarrow over his head. *Sadie* was blown ashore on West Summerland, but her crew all swam to safety. Both boats were recovered and refitted by the F.E.C., and *Sybil* was back in service in 1910.

Launches

The F.E.C. owned many launches—large and small gasoline-powered, propeller-driven craft— used for general-purpose movements of supervisory staff and workers. They were faster than the steamers and generally drew much less water. Most of them were fitted out as workboats, but a few were quite plush and were used for official visits by Henry Flagler and the upper-level F.E.C. staff.

The following list of launches includes only the ones for which known documentation and published specifications exist.

Aha	*Lucile*
Bird	*Margaret*
Bonito	*Marguerite*
City of Key West (41 ft.)	*Marjorie* (36 ft.)
	Mayflower
Clydrick	*M. S. Moreno*
Corrine (44 ft.)	*Mystery*
Dixie	*Nan*
Eagle (40 ft.)	*Nancy*
Edna (33 ft.)	*Nanette*
Ellen	*Nat*
El Moro	*Olivette*
Emala (38 ft.)	*Oriole*
Empire	*Palm*
Enterprise	*Petral*
Estelle	*Pocahontas*
Eulane	*Princess Issena* (84 ft.)
Everglade	
Florida	*Radium*
Fortune	*Sally*
Golita	*Sarah*
Hazel (40 ft.)	*Seagull* (29 ft.)
Hobo (27 ft.)	*Seattle*
Hudson	*Seminole*
Ida Belle Lounds (44 ft.)	*Skipjack*
	Stella
Idaho	*Stranger*
Irene Albury	*Three Sisters* (42 ft.)
Junior	
Lady Lou	*Wapiti*
Little Dog	*Wasp*
Lorcy (26 ft.)	*Yvette*
Lotus (78 ft.)	*Yvonne*
Louise	

Fig. 52. Launch *Dixie* near Jewfish Creek. (Museums at Crane Point Hammock)

Lotus and *Princess Issena* were much larger than average. Sporting grand cabins and posh overnight accommodations, they were used for carrying high-ranking officials on inspection tours down the Keys. They had generators and full lighting inside and out. *Princess Issena* was powered by a 50-horsepower, 4-cylinder engine. *Lotus*, acquired in September 1906, also had a 50-horsepower engine and cruised at 12 mph. *Lotus* was chosen for use by the paymaster and as the operating vessel for Chief Engineer Meredith. She had accommodations for eight passengers in staterooms.

Most of the other launches were not so elegant, having rudimentary cabins. By today's standards, they were not very powerful or fast. For example, launch *Three Sisters*, 42 feet long, was powered by an 18-horsepower engine. *Eagle*, a 40-foot vessel, had a gasoline engine rated at 10 horsepower, and the 36-foot *Lorcy* had a 6-horsepower engine that swung a 24-inch propeller.

Launch *Ida Belle Lounds*, a vessel in service throughout the project, was the victim of a freak

Fig. 53. Launch *Lucile* on left, *Nan* in the middle, and *Lotus* closest to the barge loaded with rock. (Historical Museum of South Florida)

Fig. 54. The elegant *Princess Issena*. (Historical Museum of South Florida)

Fig. 55. Launch *Nan*. This was the boat used by Krome as he kept track of progress up and down the line. (Historical Museum of South Florida)

Fig. 56. Launch *Palm*. Floating pile driver is in background. (Museums at Crane Point Hammock)

Fig. 57. Launch *Ida Belle Lounds*. Two dynamite houses are on barges in the background. (Museums at Crane Point Hammock)

accident. On November 1, 1911, while transporting workers at the Pacet Channel Viaduct, the vessel crossed behind stern-wheel steamer *Kennedy*. *Kennedy* was in reverse. The *Lounds* was proceeding out of harm's way when she ran aground, leaving her in the path of the backing steamer. *Kennedy's* paddlewheel smashed down on the hapless *Lounds*, damaging her badly and breaking five of the blades of *Kennedy's* wheel. Most of the workers jumped overboard; one who did not was badly injured and died at the hospital in Marathon within a day. Both *Lounds* and *Kennedy* were refit at the Boot Key Harbor facility.

Barges/Lighters

There is no accurate count of the number of barges or lighters in service to the F.E.C. during the construction project. Partial records list 46 barges; however, the craft were named by number, and the numbers on the list range from 28 to 150, with many numbers not accounted for on the F.E.C. roster. Because the project required moving great quantities of material over water, then transferring material from offshore steamers to shallow land bases, the flat-bottom barge was the workhorse of the fleet.

There appear to be several classes of barges. *Interstate* and *Intrastate*, two of the largest listed, were 38 feet wide and 157 feet long, making them bigger than the steamers that pushed them. Numerous smaller barges were listed at 30 feet by 100 feet. The F.E.C. ordered barges built in wholesale lots; the Southern Shipbuilding Company in Jacksonville built 28 in the spring of 1906. The smallest class of barges, measuring only 20 feet wide by 55 feet long, were possibly used in the construction of the spandrel arches for many of the bridges in the keys. A barge larg-

Fig. 58. Generic barge used for hauling many kinds of materials. Workers are unloading railroad ties from this barge at Lake Surprise near Key Largo. (Museums at Crane Point Hammock)

er than 20 feet in beam would not have been able to fit between the piers.

Almost all of the barges were made of wood. A number of detailed plans show that they were very sturdily built, with four- by six-inch floor timbers and three-inch planking. Most appear to have been round-chined, with tapered sterns and a rake to the bow. Displacement is not provided in the specifications, but the medium-sized barges carried train engines on deck at times. All were flat-bottomed, drawing as little water as possible. Some were designed for specific tasks, such as transporting sand or rock, others with tanks for water. Most were general-purpose barges with flat, open decks. A few of the larger barges had substantial deckhouses.

Cement Mixers

Cement mixers were the most intricate piece of machinery built by the F.E.C. at the Terminal Docks. These great machines were floating factories, designed to run day and night, mixing and lifting concrete to fill the forms for the piers and arches of the concrete bridges. The first one was built in 1906, and while the F.E.C. originally planned to build six of them, it apparently made ten before the project was complete.

A cement mixer began as a barge that was a bit wider than the standard work barge. It was built to carry a mixing drum and two sets of cranes. One set of cranes loaded sand, crushed rock, and cement; the other derrick controlled a large bucket that transferred wet concrete to the top of the forms to be filled. All of these devices were powered by a large steam engine fueled with

Fig. 59. Upper level crew on a cement mixer. These crew members were concerned with putting the buckets of concrete in the proper place, and loading the raw materials for the concrete. The upper deck crew operated the two sets of cranes on each mixer. (Wright Langley Archives)

Fig. 60. Two cement mixers at work on the Long Key Viaduct. The derrick on the near side operates the concrete transfer bucket; the derrick on the far side loads rock, sand, and cement. (Museums at Crane Point Hammock)

Fig. 61. Dredge *Babcock* working in Tavernier Creek, photo dated March 1, 1906. The pipeline on pontoons (left) is carrying the slurry to the dump point. (Museums at Crane Point Hammock)

coal, and the machines demanded great quantities of fuel and fresh water when in operation. These mixers were also equipped with electric dynamos so that they could run day and night.

Cement mixers had a large crew consisting of firemen, deckhands, and the more specialized derrick operators. There were no "captains"; these vessels were moved from place to place by tugs since they had no motive power of their own. Since they were steam-powered, there was always a stationary engineer on board in charge of the engine.

As concrete was mixed and transported to the waiting forms, samples were taken periodically to ascertain that the mixture was of good quality. These samples were poured into small forms, then transported to labs for testing. Knight's Key Dock and Pigeon Key both had concrete test labs.

Dredges

Since the project required that great amounts of fill be moved, a number of dredges were built for this purpose at the Terminal Docks. The total number of dredges acquired is unknown, but in May 1907, there were 13 of them working. Dredges were built on barges and were of two types—"suction" dredges and "orange peel" dredges. Each had a large steam engine as the working heart of the machine.

Hydraulic or suction dredges mounted a boom on the front with a bucket that could dig up sand and loose sediment and deposit it in a hopper. A powerful pump then forced the sediments as a slurry of water and mud through large-diameter pipes. These pipes were supported on pontoons and were somewhat flexible so that the dredge could move around for new material without "re-plumbing" the whole system. When the stream of water and sediment dumped in the spoil area, it settled to make new land.

Suction dredges operated where the bottom was marshy; they were not designed to chip away at coral bedrock. For this job it was necessary to use orange-peel dredges, which also had an additional boom that carried a bucket out to the far

Fig. 62. Dredge *Mikado* building the roadbed at Lake Surprise. Here the dredge is working like an excavator with a clamshell bucket. (Museums at Crane Point Hammock)

Fig. 63. Suction dredge *Oyama* at work, site unknown. The long pipeline on pontoons trails behind to the dump area. (Historical Museum of South Florida)

Fig. 64. Dredge *Prickly Heat* at work in Lake Surprise, June 1906. (Museums at Crane Point Hammock)

Fig. 65. Dredge *Rough Rider* on the railways at Boot Key Harbor Machine Shop. (Monroe County Public Library)

Fig. 66. Dredge *Grampus*. In this photo *Grampus* is rigged with a bucket, and is working at the Trumbo fill site in Key West. (Monroe County Public Library)

Fig. 67. Dredge *George W. Allen* working in Key West at the Trumbo fill. (Monroe County Public Library)

length of travel, dropped the bucket, and hauled it back to the barge. Teeth on the bucket chewed layers from the coral bedrock or marl pits. The full bucket was hauled above the water and dumped to create fill.

Two dredges were purchased in the summer of 1906 to work in Key West. The *Grampus* cost the F.E.C. $40,000 and needed to be rebuilt as soon as it was purchased. The second dredge, *Texas City*, was renamed the *George W. Allen* after the F.E.C. bought it. Both vessels worked extensively in Key West, dredging land for Trumbo Point. On April 15, 1907, the boiler on the *Allen* exploded at 4:00 A.M. Two firemen were killed;

seven others were injured by steam. The *George W. Allen* was not extensively damaged and was repaired for future work in Key West.

Dredges were general-purpose machines as well. Because they were equipped with derricks, they could move materials with buckets or with crane hooks. When the dredges were not doing dredging operations, they moved marl, rock, earth, sand, and other materials.

Derrick Barges

Many of the working barges sported derricks, which were small cranes specialized for the work they did. The derrick barges were built especially

Fig. 68. *Derrick Barge No. 9* rigged with an extra long boom. It was designed especially to raise the steel deck plates from train cars or barges to the level of the piers on the Knight's Key Bridge. This photograph is at the Tail Track Dock in Marathon. (Monroe County Public Library)

Fig 69. Two derricks on a single barge. This rig is needed to get the large cofferdam off the barge. (Monroe County Public Library)

for lifting. The booms and frames for these vessels were made entirely of wood; the hoisting mechanisms and drums were powered by steam engines. The barges were built at the Terminal Docks; one under construction in March 1907 was rated at 15 tons. When there were exceptionally heavy objects to be lifted (such as large cofferdams), a pair of derrick barges worked together.

Pile Drivers

It is estimated that more than 200,000 pilings were set into the bottom of Florida Bay during the construction project. The F.E.C. built a number of floating pile drivers that were towed into position to first hammer holes into the coral bedrock, then drive pilings to anchor cofferdams, support arch forms, and provide support for docks and trestles. The largest pile drivers dropped their hammer 70 feet. The hammer was raised with steam power, then released to run down guides and punch the piling into the coral

bedrock. Records show that the F.E.C. built at least eight of these floating pile drivers by early 1907. Two were lost at Long Key in the hurricane on October 17, 1906. The pile drivers moved from site to site, spending a year or more at the Long Key project, then moving down to the Knight's Key Bridge project after 1908.

Other Specialized Craft

Anticipating wrecks and sunk vessels, the F.E.C. converted Steamer *Satilla* to salvage machinery as necessary from unfortunate watercraft. The *Satilla,* also called a "snag boat," was fitted with booms and winches to lift boilers and other heavy machinery from the bottom. In March 1907, *Satilla* and crew salvaged machinery from four cement mixers and two pile drivers lost in the October 1906 hurricane that devastated Long Key.

A number of barges were designed especially to carry water. *Mikado*, for example, at 41 feet long and 12 feet wide, had a large wooden tank

Fig. 70. Pile driver barge working at Knight's Key Dock. (Museums at Crane Point Hammock)

Fig. 71. Snag boat *Satilla*. This was a specialized stern wheel steamer. (Historical Museum of South Florida)

built inside the barge with the deck over the tank. The tank itself was 5 feet by 21 feet, and 2.5 feet deep (262.5 cubic feet). Other barges had tanks on deck, some as large as 1,100 cubic feet.

Prior to February 1907 any vessel or equipment needing repairs was brought back to the Terminal Docks in Miami; there were no machine shops in the Keys. To solve this problem, the Terminal Docks shipwrights built a huge floating machine shop on a barge and sent it down to the Long Key site, where several cement mixers, pile drivers, and other craft were hard at work. In April 1908, a large machine shop opened at Boot Key Harbor; presumably the floating machine shop was decommissioned at this point.

While not a F.E.C. vessel, the *Sanator* was an old screw-powered steamer of a thousand tons, with a relatively deep draft. In 1909 the vessel served as a U.S. quarantine ship; a Dr. Porter was the physician in charge. *Sanator* was washed ashore in Boot Key Harbor by the hurricane of 1909. It was irretrievably stranded, and served as a boathouse and commissary until it was destroyed by fire and was declared a total loss. The hulk was reported still on the shoreline of Boot Key in 1917.

Fig. 72. *Sanator* washed ashore on Boot Key during the hurricane of 1909. (Historical Museum of South Florida)

4

The Workers

WHILE ENGINEERS DID THE PLANNING and dreaming, the Extension progressed because laborers bent their backs and blistered their hands and feet. Ultimately the project came down to men, brawny and scrawny, swinging hammers, pushing pencils, and moving incredible amounts of water, steel, rock, sand, and marl. They shifted the surface of the earth to make it suit the needs of the railway. It was hard labor under the fierce subtropical conditions of a wild part of America.

The workers came from the U.S. and other countries. In the early years, many came from east coast cities such as New York and Philadelphia. A worker received credit for transportation down to the Extension ($12.50 from Philadelphia) and could work this off in three months. Pay for laborers was $1.25 per day, with food and housing provided at a cost of 40 cents per day; the worker had the option of refusing to pay board. Salaried workers earned $75 per month.

Fig. 73. A crew of rough workers operating the floating cement mixer take a break for a posed photograph. (Wright Langley Archives)

Fig. 74. Worker housing. Platform tents such as these were considered luxury housing and were common in the permanent camps. (Curtis Skomp)

Fig. 75. Workers from Pigeon Key Camp unloading timbers under the growing Pigeon Key Bridge. (Wright Langley Archives)

In May 1906, wages for laborers were raised to $1.50 per day; carpenters with their own tools received $2.50 per day. Foremen and salaried workers also got raises; they now earned $85 per month. Black and white workers were paid equally.

The beliefs of Americans at the turn of the century included the idea that races and ethnic groups had distinctly different abilities. Black workers were considered capable of cutting and clearing operations for the right-of-way but were not suitable for earth-moving operations, carpentry, or other skilled jobs. White laborers—notably Greeks, Italians, and Germans—were destined to be the movers of earth. There are no records of any black workers at foreman or management levels. During the summer months fewer white workers were hired; more black workers filled their places during the hot weather. It was thought at the time that the blacks did better in the heat of the summer. In July 1906, for example, there were about 700 white workers and 1,000 black workers in the Keys.

While some work camps included a mixture of nationalities, other camps contained a single ethnic group. An article from the *St. Lucie Tribune* in 1905 notes:

> There are some six thousand men in camp scattered from the mainland to Key West, some cutting out right-of-way, building the grades and others on dredges building embankments across the waterways. An interesting feature of the work is the division of the races into separate camps. One camp especially, composed of New York Indians, presents a unique picture, and they seem thoroughly familiar with their work.

The company paid workers monthly in gold coin. The F.E.C. sent payroll down by boat in the early years; as the tracks lengthened, management sent money down by train to settlements on the main line. In December 1907, the F.E.C. gave all workmen in the Keys a day off with full pay on Christmas. Newspapers were quick to point out that, with more than two thousand workers on the payroll at the time,

Extension Song

This ditty appeared in print as a tribute to the workers on the project.

The Extension!
Sing a song of the swinging sledge
Steel to Steel!
Keeping time to the throb
Of a pumping dredge
With mud sucked keel.
Building a road where the
Stone crabs hide
Chaining the flow of
Restless tide
Crossing the marsh
Where Gators bide
With the crush of an iron wheel!
                              Crain.

Key West Citizen,
December 20, 1906

Fig. 76. Workers gathered in front of their tents at Camp No. 12 on Stock Island. Two of the workers are getting shaved. The construction crews worked six days a week with Sunday off; it is likely that this photograph was taken on a Sunday. (Historical Museum of South Florida)

the gift represented considerable F.E.C. cash at the current wage rate.

Work Camps

The nature of the construction project necessitated two different types of work camps, temporary and permanent. Temporary camps were most common in the early years when it was important for groups of workers to be moving down the line as they built up the grade. These workers were the ones clearing the jungle and moving coral rock and sand for the roadbed. With this kind of work there was little need for professional staff other than the general foreman in the field. The camps were rough, generally tent camps with outdoor cooking and eating facilities. There was no transportation other than by foot or boat since there was no track in place.

Life in these camps was without amenities

such as running water, good kitchens, or table service. Men had little protection from insects, sun, or inclement weather. They labored six days a week, and when Sunday arrived, they had little to do out in the wilds of the Keys. It was a good day for haircuts and writing letters home. If the workers could get a boat to Key West or Miami, they made the most of their day off in these towns. Many workers gambled as a recreational activity and lost much of what they earned on the job.

Miami loved the brawny laborers who passed through on their way to the Extension— and hoped they would pass through town on their way out. The workers contributed to the economy of the town, since there were as many as two or three thousand workers at a time in the Keys. Police kept their eyes on the workers and generally restricted them to the part of town near the Terminal Docks. Newspaper reports

Few Laborers Who Leave Extension
Get Further Away Than To Miami
Spend All Their Money Here, Can't Get Home, and Return
To The Keys Where They Are Re-Employed.

Quite a crowd of former extension laborers were about the city today, awaiting pay day that they can get what money is coming to them. When this has been done, some few will leave for points north ostensibly for their homes, while the very great majority will wend their way to a groggery and there remain until the cop scoops them in or their money is gone. Then they will begin to cast around for a morsel of food and a couch for sleep. Neither comes very readily and as a last resort they will re-ship to the extension and spend several more long months accumulating wealth, then coming up to the city again to spend it.

As a foreman of the extension works said this morning, "The greater majority of these men have no desire or intention of going back north. They know they are better treated and receive better wages in the keys than they ever received in their lives. They simply want to get off for a rest or recreating, and we know and can count upon fully 90 percent of the number leaving the works coming back again, just as soon as they have been to Miami and spent all their money."

Times Union, March 14, 1907

Fig. 77. Workers in luxury quarters at the permanent Pigeon Key Camp. There were four big dorms like this one; each dorm slept 64 workers. (Museums at Crane Point Hammock)

Fig. 78. Marathon School, 1910 or 1911. This one-room school building was located a few feet from the main line, and it must have been very noisy when trains passed by. (Wright Langley Archives)

were sometimes cynical, such as this excerpt from the *Times-Union* on March 14, 1907:

> Several camps became permanent, such as those at Bahia Honda, Long Key, Pigeon Key, and Marathon. The engineers planned the major camps from the beginning, knowing they would need a long-term presence in the area. The camp at Marathon, for example, began in 1906 and was still in use in 1916. The permanent camps were quite comfortable. Some included wooden buildings for human comfort and for storage. They had cooking facilities, sewage disposal, dormitories, single houses, a medical station, a commissary, and a post office. Although tents for the workers remained, they were on sturdy platforms, raised from the ground.

Life for the salaried workers was much better than for the common laborers, especially at camps that operated continuously for several years and became communities. Foremen were allowed to bring their families to the Keys for the greater part of the year, but women and children were made to leave during hurricane season. The railroad did not provide housing for families, but numerous salaried employees built cabins or houseboats for their families. In Marathon the community of salaried

Fig. 79. Chief Bridge Tender R.T. Kyle in his front yard at Pigeon Key. (Robert and Melanie Frentzel)

workers grew so large that the F.E.C. provided a schoolhouse. In 1910 there were 16 children enrolled.

After the railway began operating on a regular basis, the company built housing for permanent employees like bridge tenders and section foremen. Pigeon Key still has a few of these buildings. The F.E.C. encouraged salaried employees to have their families with them, hoping to get stable, long-term committed staff. At Pigeon Key, for example, Robert Kyle, his wife Leona, and their six children lived in a F.E.C. house from 1912 until 1927. Kyle, as chief bridge tender on Pigeon Key, Kyle enjoyed free housing and a salary of $90 per month in 1912.

Securing Labor

In the beginning, the F.E.C. had difficulty finding good laborers for the Extension project even though their wages of $1.25 per day were about 25 cents higher than the average U.S. rate at the time. Recruiters in New York, Philadelphia, and other east coast cities found that their advertisements appealed to many unsuitable applicants, and they weeded out some at initial interviews. Workers signed contracts with the F.E.C. when they agreed to come to the Keys. The contract charged them for their transportation from their point of origin to Jacksonville; this amount was subtracted from their pay during the first three months of their employment. If they quit before they paid the money off, they owed the company. And if they quit, they had to pay $1.50 for transport back to Miami.

However a number of undesirable workers sneaked in—some just for a ride to warm weather—and they became liabilities when they faced the reality of harsh life in the Keys. Many poten-

Fig. 80. New crew of workers arriving in the Keys. (Museums at Crane Point Hammock)

tial workers took the train as far as Jacksonville, jumped off, and went to work as farmhands. Some arrived in Miami, and then decided they wanted out, but did not fare well. Miami police and hired guards assumed that any person not employed was a vagrant and arrested him. Some of the workers ended up on chain gangs for the State of Florida.

Once the laborers reached the Keys, they were distributed to camps as necessary. The company encouraged good workers to stay on and fired those who wouldn't work. Fired workers are often disgruntled workers; some of them may well have contributed to the peonage stories that began to emerge from the Extension.

In 1906 stories began circulating that the workers in the Keys were brutally abused, that the F.E.C. used deceptive hiring practices to lure the workers to the Keys, and that they were held against their will, unable to return home. Some stories reported that the workers were not paid, had no beds, and were starved. There were rumors that recruiters got young men drunk and put them in southbound trains; they woke up in Jacksonville under guard, bound for the Keys. The more lurid stories reported that Negroes with whips and guns stood guard over the laborers. Headlines spoke of "White Slavery in the South." It was a classic case of yellow journalism, and each newspaper tried to outdo the others with scandalous details.

The agencies that the F.E.C. hired to recruit workers may have been overzealous in their mission. The agencies were paid $2 for every worker they sent down to Jacksonville. One lawsuit accused an agent of misrepresenting the salary and the travel conditions to the Keys. No F.E.C. employees were charged with misleading workers about salaries or conditions.

From all accounts, the F.E.C. and Henry Flagler were highly offended by these stories. The company felt that it had sincerely tried to do the best it could for the workers. It marshaled its forces (and newspapers) for counterattacks and provided stories of its own to show how great it was to work in the Keys.

A classic battle of the press followed. New York newspapers broke the stories first, claiming they had interviewed some former Extension workers from their cities who brought them reports of abuse. Other newspapers embraced different sides of the peonage issue. The *Philadelphia Inquirer* sent down an investigative reporter who found no problems with the camps, no stories of brutality, no foremen with guns, just healthy living conditions and happy workers. The *Chicago Daily News* reported the same from their own investigations. The whole notion of abuse should have disappeared as rumors do, but somehow the subject stayed alive long enough to draw the attention of the courts.

A New York federal grand jury indicted the F.E.C. and gathered affidavits and witnesses to substantiate the peonage claims. In late 1908, the case was tried and was settled by a judge, who directed the jury to return a verdict of acquittal. The judge rebuked the prosecution for bringing such a flimsy case made up of hearsay evidence to his courtroom. The ruling put an end to all of the stories, and the peonage issue never came up again.

In fact, there was little or no brutality towards the workers in the camps. Foremen were not allowed to have guns, and any foreman found to be brutal was instantly discharged. At times the workers seemed to have the upper hand. If they didn't want to go out of the camp on a given day, they stayed in with no penalty, except for loss of a day's pay. Occasionally a work crew would go on strike if, for example, a foreman fired a popular worker. The strikes generally lasted for one day; on the next day all of the laborers were back.

Weekly Work Reports

Resident engineers at each camp prepared weekly work reports that summarized progress on the construction project. The reports included a summary of the work force at the camp. The report below, submitted by Resident Engineer C. S. Coe for the Pigeon Key Camp, shows the distribution of the types of workers for the bridge construction project. While there were some professional and managerial workers, most were common laborers.

Work force at Pigeon Key Camp
Week ending January 29, 1910

Engineering and Accounting	18
Foremen	13
Subsistence	28
Launchmen	12
Skilled labor	27
Common labor	189
Total	*287*

Fig. 81. Butchers at Pigeon Key pose with the tools of their trade. (Wright Langley Archives)

The total of 287 men on Pigeon Key may seem like a large number for such a small island, but there were often more than 400 men quartered there. In October of 1909, the weekly work report shows 467 workers.

In 1910 the U.S. Census recorded important information about the workers on Pigeon Key, including data on ages, birthplaces, and job titles. Most of the force on Pigeon Key at the time was unskilled labor. On the day of the census, there were 211 people counted on the island. Sixty-one were U.S. born; the remaining 150 were from foreign shores. Thirty-three hailed from Grand Cayman, 77 from Spain. The remainder were a mixture from ten other countries, including 13 from Ireland. Almost all of the foreign workers were unskilled common laborers. Only five workers were black.

The job titles reveal the distribution of skill levels at the bridge-building camp. At the upper level, with management and decision-making power, were the engineers. Specific job titles included engineer, civil engineer, engineer/pile driver, engineer/derrick barge, engineer/concrete, structural iron worker, carpenter, carpenter/concrete forms, foreman/cement mixer, iron worker, and stevedore foreman.

A number of the workers were in service professions, including janitors, housekeepers, orderlies, and one laundress. Specific job titles included cook, waiter, steward/cook, storekeeper, baker, kitchen hand, butcher, watchman, timekeeper, and fireman.

Many employees were in the marine trades, charged with moving men and materials from place to place. Related job titles included boatman, tugboat pilot, launch captain, deck hand, pile driver deck hand, catamaran deck hand, and pile driver mate.

A MIGHTY WORK FORCE

Although newspaper accounts describing the number of workers employed in the Keys vary widely, the annual reports for the F.E.C. detailed the numbers, reporting the minimum, maximum, and average during each fiscal year. Generally the maximum numbers were during the winter months, and minimums were during summer and the hurricane season.

Figure 75 shows that the peak employment period was during 1911–1912, just before the opening of the Extension to regular traffic. An average of 2,500 workers were on the job, with a maximum of 3,626 showing on the payroll in November 1911. Another peak time is in 1906–1907, when the initial roadbed through the Keys was built. After the trains began to run in 1912, the work force gradually decreased but was still significant while the engineers and laborers finished the last bridges and raised the grade on much of the line. While half of the earth was moved in the last four years (see Fig. 20), there were many fewer laborers doing this work. At this time great quantities of marl and rock were quarried and hauled by mechanical means. Excavators and Goodwin cars replaced the laborer to a great extent, saving the project money while moving more material for the roadbed.

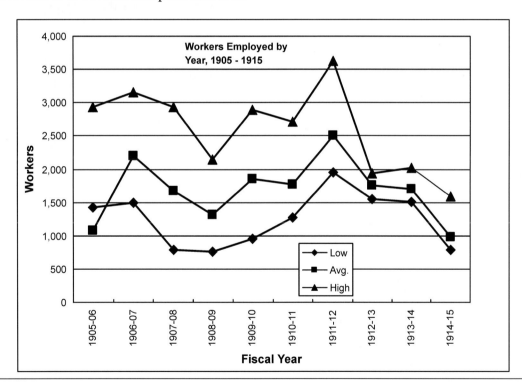

While many of the workers had these kinds of specialty tasks, most employees on the census were listed simply as "laborer."

Medical Care

When a worker was injured, he would first be sent to the nearest camp with a medical staff person. Large camps, such as those on Long Key, Marathon, and Key West, had staff doctors or male nurses to provide medical services. If the disease or injury was beyond the scope of the camp service, the afflicted worker was sent to Miami (at no charge) for help at the official F.E.C. hospital. Dr. James M. Jackson Jr., one of

Fig. 82. Hospital in Marathon. Doc Lowe is on the steps with his medical bag. (Wright Langley Archives)

Fig. 83. Hospital tent on Pigeon Key. Doc Lowe is in the center with vest and bowler. (Wright Langley Archives)

the leading physicians in the state, was in charge at the Miami F.E.C. hospital.

The field hospitals were fairly spartan. Pigeon Key, for example, had a hospital inside a tent. Edward R. Lowe, a nurse, was in charge of the hospital at Marathon but made trips to Pigeon Key, where he oversaw health services at the tent.

The company was very proactive on health matters. A 1907 memo from General Manager J. R. Parrott to J. S. Meredith reads:

> As summer is coming on I want to impress upon you the necessity of screen-ing the kitchen and dining rooms, taking care of all waste water around each camp.
>
> Flies are the greatest medium of carrying disease that we know of, and this is through the food. It does not make any difference whether the camp is a temporary one or permanent camp, but if care is taken in putting up the screens they can be taken down from temporary camps and used at other places, using what may be termed a portable screen.
>
> Please see that instructions are given on this line at once and that the same are carried out.

In spite of the tropical conditions and hostile environment of the Keys, there are no records of any disease outbreaks during the construction project. Indeed, some workers reported that they were healthier working on the Extension than in past jobs. One worker reported that the work was not as hard as he had experienced on the tunnel excavations in New York City. He did not have to risk his life with cave-ins, there was no snow, and while he was able to work every day in Florida, the dampness of the tunnel work in New York City kept him from his labor one or two days a week.

ALCOHOL

Demon rum stories appear throughout the construction effort. The brawny field workers were from a rough-and-tumble construction world where alcohol was a part of their life. W. R. Hawkins, who kept a diary about working conditions during the construction years, reports in his journal that he had to fire three of his machine shop staff because their work "has been unsatisfactory for some time due to too much liquor."

Alcohol was forbidden in the work camps but somehow always seemed to be available. Whisky cost $5 per quart, a sizeable portion of a paycheck. Generally it was brought into the camps by enterprising waterborne bootleggers. Hawkins mentions in his journal the "terrible Knight brothers from Key West who sold liquor from boats." The company put a guard on Pigeon Key authorized to shoot at boats approaching at night if he suspected that they were bootleggers. Hawkins was proactive in preventing alcohol from coming into Marathon; his diary records that he spent October 24, 1909, "watching for booze boat part of A.M. and P.M."

In September 1908 some railroad staff and officials gathered at Long Key for a meeting to plan for hurricanes. At this time two wildcat liquor dealers, Charles Hammond and John Allen, brought down a large quantity of booze and distributed it widely throughout the area. At Central Supply, so many of the dredge crews imbibed that they were unable to operate their vessels; this scene was repeated at lower Matecumbe. On Long Key, the liquor dealers had a very successful day selling booze to two groups of Spanish workers, causing much disorder in Camp No. 9. The railway officials at the meeting were irate when they learned of the mayhem around them. They captured Hammond and Allen at Long Key and destroyed their boat and liquor. Somehow the prisoners "got away" during the night. The next day a search party found an empty tar bucket and a broken pillow—the pair had evidently seen some local justice.

It was risky drinking some of the bootlegger's potions. In July 1907, two workers died from "Tiger Booze," which they purchased from four whiskey salesmen who visited the Long Key camp by boat from Key West. The bootleggers were jailed and charged with murder. One newspaper observed, "This case may lead to the extermination of these floating rum shops which have been a real detriment to the work of the F.E.C. Extension."

The Extension project was under way during the years of the temperance movement in the U.S. Whether or not it is true that alcohol interfered with construction is unclear. The workers probably drank less than they wanted because of company-imposed restrictions but drank more than their supervisors wished.

Deaths and Injuries

Whenever great structures are built, planners know that there will be accidents and deaths, no matter how many safeguards are in place. In the construction of the F.E.C. Key West Extension the scope of the work offered many chances for mishap. The workers were in an alien environment, isolated from rapid medical assistance. There were poisonous snakes, alligators, scorpions, and other dangerous life forms in the Keys. The project lay in the path of Atlantic hurricanes. And the work itself placed men at risk. At times the workers were below the water, at other times high above it. They operated steam-powered machinery with heat and high-pressure boilers. They moved heavy material. Accidents were bound to happen, and they did.

There are no firm figures on how many workers were killed or injured during the Extension project. The best source (and a conservative one) comes from reading all of the newspaper articles covering the period. The news media were focused on the project and reported accidents and deaths as they happened.

The unofficial death toll during the construction period comes to

---

HURRICANE OF 1906 AT LONG KEY

On October 17, 1906, a hurricane struck the construction site at Long Key. It was by all accounts a mild hurricane, with winds of 80 mph reported officially. However, this storm caused the greatest loss of life of any single tragedy on the Extension project.

At this time the first 13 piers at the east end of the Long Key Viaduct were complete but had no arches built. *Quarterboat No. 4*, home to 131–160 workers (sources vary), was tethered to 16 pilings in the same area. The boat was torn from its moorings by winds or storm surge at night. Although reports and affidavits conflict, the boat apparently broke up when it crashed into several of the completed piers as it was swept out to sea. Some men were killed at this time, many more drowned subsequently. Survivors clung to the wreckage through the night, and passing ships in the Gulf Stream picked up many in the following days. One newspaper reported that 49 survivors were picked up clinging to the hulk of the houseboat off Cape Sable and brought to Key West. Another vessel picked up 24 men and took them to Savannah. Three survivors were taken all the way to England before they could return. The best estimates gave the final death toll at about 100 men lost, with 76 known survivors. While this was not the worst hurricane to strike the project, it was by far the deadliest.

As a result of the storm and deaths, the F.E.C. determined that quarterboats, while convenient, were unsafe in storms, and the company began to build most of their housing on land. They also began building hurricane canals at many of their sites, which afforded sheltered areas for their work barges in case of storms.

Fig. 84. Hurricane warning flags fly over Marathon on October 9, 1909. (Monroe County Public Library)

158 men killed, and another 81 were injured while working. While this may seem to be a great number of deaths, most occurred on the day of the 1906 hurricane that swept Quarterboat 4 out to sea and also sank the *St. Lucie.* An estimated 100 men died from the quarterboat sinking, and 20 more from the *St. Lucie* wreck. In the 1909 hurricane, 11 men died when the tugboat *Sybil* went down at Bahia Honda, and another man drowned in Marathon. Hurricanes were responsible for 132 of the 158 deaths reported.

The second-greatest cause of death and injury involved mishaps with dynamite. Three isolated accidents in the upper Keys killed four people. One of them, on Plantation Key, may have been a murder; a fuse was found leading to the decedent's tent. Two of them were a father and his son working at Quarry.

In mid-May 1909, seven workers were killed and one foreman and six laborers seriously injured in a premature dynamite explosion at the west end of Cudjoe Key. The men were a part of a gang of seventeen laborers staying on Quarterboat 3. They had loaded a number of

Fig. 85. Dynamite, a powerful construction tool, was used daily on the Extension project. It is amazing that so few accidents resulted from explosions. (Steele)

underwater holes with dynamite earlier in the day. While several theories of what went wrong were suggested, management was never able to come to a conclusion. The dead and injured were taken to Key West.

The worst dynamite accident took place in 1909 at the Boca Chica camp when ten workers died and nine were seriously injured. According to the *Key West Citizen*, about 50 workers were in the area. One of the workers noticed that a 50-pound box of dynamite was burning on a platform. He shouted to his coworkers, then jumped from a scaffold into the water, but his warning was too late. The box exploded and, in what must have been a chain reaction, ignited other charges that the men had placed during the day as well as other dynamite lying around. The foreman estimated that 700 pounds of dynamite exploded in that brutal moment. Dynamite accidents killed a total of 21 workers and maimed another dozen during the course of the Extension project.

The remaining fatalities resulted from a variety of causes—mishaps with schooner booms, falls from trestles, and workers crushed between boats and burned by gasoline fires

aboard boats. Alcohol may have been involved with some deaths; one worker was sleeping on the track and was run over by a train.

There are no accounts of accidents specific to Florida—no deaths of divers by drowning or decompression sickness, and no deaths from snakebites, sharks, or alligators. There are no anecdotes of men buried alive in concrete pours or crushed by falling steel. No deaths are attributed to tropical diseases; this suggests that camp management followed the F.E.C. health precautions for cleanliness and insect screening. Resident Engineer C. S. Coe reported that no workers died from accidents during the construction of the Knight's Key—Little Duck crossing or the Bahia Honda Bridge. From the data on hand, we must conclude that the Extension project was relatively safe, probably much safer than subway or skyscraper construction. The company was alert for problems, with a medical infrastructure in place to deal with them. If it had not been for two hurricanes, the death toll would have been minimal—85 percent of the deaths on the Key West Extension construction project happened in two storms.

5

Homestead to Snake Creek

IN 1904 PRESIDENT THEODORE ROOSEVELT was in the White House. The economy was strong. The Wright brothers had recently demonstrated that air flight was possible. The St. Louis World Fair showcased the growing use of electricity for new and wonderful products and utopian ways of living. Cross-ocean traffic on steamers was almost as common as air travel today, and waves of immigrants flooded the east and west coasts of America. The country was growing rapidly, and progress and change were not considered radical but the status quo. At this time trains were as commonplace in most of America as buses are today. By the end of 1904 the surveyors had completed their initial rough work for the Extension route, and workers began construction in April 1905. Beginning a new rail extension line seemed like a normal outgrowth of the American dream.

Homestead to Jewfish Creek
While work was under way at many sites in the Keys in 1905, the first rail section completed connected Homestead to Jewfish Creek. This was a critical first step in order to shorten the over-water supply lines. For this, the engineers needed webbed feet—the route was over 20 miles of Everglades terrain. Swamps and sawgrass covered the route; it was half water and half land.

Workers used boom and orange-peel buckets for this work. The bucket, swung forward of the barge by the long boom, sank to the bottom. Then power from the drum on the excavator pulled the bucket back to the barge, filling it as it returned. The boom then picked up the full bucket, swung it over to the area to be filled, and dumped the material.

Four great excavators were built for the project. One pair started from near Homestead and progressed towards Jewfish Creek, one on each side of the proposed railway. A second pair started from Jewfish Creek and headed north. As they chewed away at the Everglades muck, they created a canal for their own passage. They dumped their spoils in the middle, forming the

Fig. 86. Floating excavator working the new fill for the Homestead-Jewfish Creek connection. In the distance (on right) is a floating quarterboat where the men lived. (Museums at Crane Point Hammock)

higher ground that became the right-of-way for the track. Some of the canals they dug on each side are still visible from the highway. There were two areas in this long passage designed for sidings; these areas were wider than the usual fill. We recognize these areas today as the designated "passing zones" on the 18-Mile Stretch.

This part of the project began in May 1905. By January 1906 the machines were making progress, and each pair had completed five miles in their respective directions. On July 1 they were within 800 yards of each other, and within

Fig. 87. Two excavators piling fill in the middle as they built the 18-mile connection between Homestead and Jewfish Creek. If the water level was too shallow to float the barges, workers pumped water from one side to the other. (Museums at Crane Point Hammock)

Fig. 88. Grading on the Homestead-Jewfish Creek connection. (Museums at Crane Point Hammock)

Fig. 89. Fill is drying out. Shortly after this a rock base is added to the fill. (Museums at Crane Point Hammock)

Fig. 90. The last step—placing ties and track on the Homestead-Jewfish connection. This photo is dated June 30, 1906. (Museums at Crane Point Hammock)

Fig. 91. North abutment at Jewfish Creek Drawbridge. Homestead is 20 miles in the distance. (Monroe County Public Library)

Fig. 92. Jewfish Drawbridge in place. The camp is on the south side of the creek on the right. The bridge at Jewfish was 99'6" long. It was designed as a deck girder swing span, and was operated by hand. A sternwheeler steamer is approaching the drawspan on the left. The tower in the center is a pile driver. (Historical Museum of South Florida)

a few days the fill was completed and ready for grading. In August work was nearly finished on a large triangular dock at Jewfish Creek that would be a major transfer station when the rails were completed to this point.

By December 1 steel rail finally reached all the way from Homestead to Jewfish Creek. Meanwhile in Miami, workers at the Terminal Docks were assembling a large steel drawspan for the Jewfish Creek Bridge. The span was complet-

ed in December and was brought down to mate with the standing spans crossing Jewfish Creek. It was evidently a difficult task to place the drawspan, and Krome called for his best practical mechanic, Ed Sherran. Unschooled in engineering but well known for his experience, Sherran took one brief look at the blueprints, then proceeded to install the span and make it work in a few days. The bridge was fully operational by February 5, 1907.

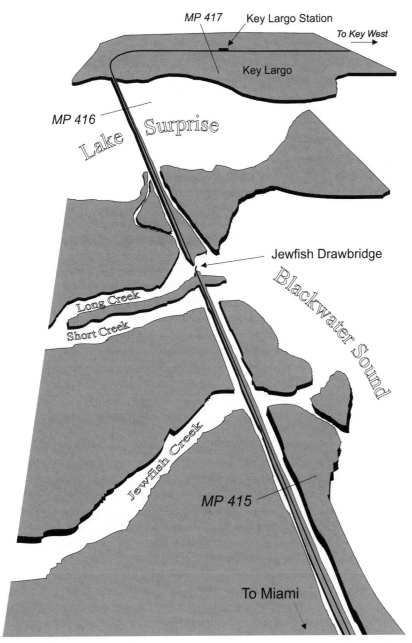

MP 417   Key Largo Station

To Key West

Key Largo

MP 416

Lake Surprise

Jewfish Drawbridge

Blackwater Sound

Long Creek

Short Creek

Jewfish Creek

MP 415

To Miami

Fig. 84. Jewfish Creek, with its two branches, Long Creek and Short Creek, were the natural connections from the Atlantic via Barnes Sound into Blackwater Sound in Florida Bay and were major waterways for small boats. If the railroad had blocked these passages, it would have impeded inter-Keys shipping, and indeed, cut off a route that the F.E.C. needed to transport much of the construction materials into Florida Bay. Thus a drawspan at this site was imperative.

Long Creek and Short Creek both fed from Jewfish Creek. The surveyors determined that Long Creek would be the best shipping channel, and blocked the western ends of Jewfish Creek and Short Creek with the right-of-way causeway. At the point where Long Creek widened, they installed the Jewfish draw spans.

At this point the F.E.C. had completed the first phase of its plan. Now materials were sent by rail directly to Jewfish Creek instead of being routed through the Miami Terminal Docks, and the supply routes by water were shortened by about 50 miles. The Miami Terminal Docks were still important as a construction facility, and some shipping still went by the long sea route. However, much of the heavy material and all of the fresh water for the Keys now left from docks at Jewfish. Engine 11 was assigned to serv-

ice between the Miami Terminal Docks and Jewfish in January 1907, and it made many runs with materials for the Keys.

The station at Jewfish (Mile post 415.5) developed just below the drawspan on the Blackwater Sound side of the track. Because of its "crossroads" location for boat and rail traffic, Jewfish saw a lot of activity and opened and closed the drawspan often.

By 1916 there was a small complex of buildings, including a residence for the bridge

MILE POSTS AND CHAINS

The F.E.C. had three ways of identifying locations along the roadbed. During construction, the entire length was broken into "sections," with Section 1 located in the Everglades near Homestead, and Section 51 including Stock Island. The sections varied in length. Section 13, for example, included the connection between Windley's Island and upper Matecumbe Key and was one of the smallest sections at only 2,596 feet long. Other sections were quite large—Section 9 included most of Plantation Key for a distance of 19,153 feet. Section designations were for the convenience of assigning work crews, but were not very precise.

The railway also published mile post designations for the convenience of train engineers and passengers. Mile Post 0 began at Jacksonville at the north end of the St. Johns River. Key West, at the other end of the track, was Mile Post 522. In the Keys, the mile post designations located the great bend at Key Largo at about MP 416.5, Tavernier Creek at MP 432, old town Marathon at MP 474, central Big Pine at MP 492 (this marker is still in place), and Shark Key at about MP 512. These mile posts do not correspond in any fashion to the current U.S. Highway 1 marking system, and in fact go in the opposite direction.

The mile post designation was not precise enough for construction engineers and surveyors, however, who relied on an extremely rigorous measure of the right-of-way in feet and inches, again based on the MP 0 in Jacksonville. Actually they measured distance with a 100-foot-long chain, and thus the measures were termed "chainings." Any distance along the roadbed was recorded as the number of 100-

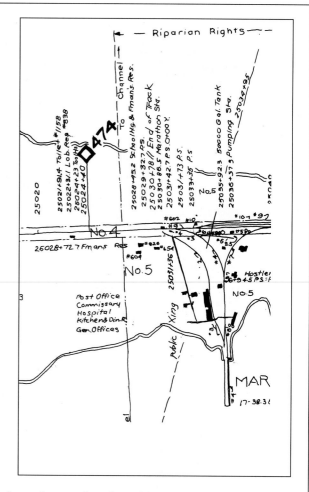

foot chains plus the additional footage. For example, the end of the line at Key West was 27570 segments of the 100-foot chain plus an additional 62 feet. This was noted on survey maps in the format 27570+62. In the accompanying figure (taken from a section of a track survey map drawn in 1916), we can see the chaining numbers precisely scribed for all of the items of interest at Mile Post 474. We can determine that toilet #1158 was located at 25021+94.1, and the Marathon Station was at 25030+86.5. If translated into feet, this means that the Marathon Station was 2,503,086.5 feet from Jacksonville; divide this by the number of feet in a mile (5,280), and the result comes to 474.06. Thus the chaining numbers correspond directly with the mile post system.

Fig. 94. Rock roadbed added to the fill across Lake Surprise. Track is completed. (Historical Museum of South Florida)

tender, one for the agent, a toilet, a platform, and other buildings. The station was at 21930+67 (see "Mile Posts and Chains" on previous page for explanation), just a couple of hundred feet south of the drawspan. All of the buildings were on the bay side of the track.

Between Jewfish and Key Largo, the workers discovered a surprise—a "lake" that the original surveyors missed or omitted from the first survey. This became known as Lake Surprise. The engineers and workers went to work with their dredges and pulled enough fill from surrounding areas to cover the 3000-foot distance.

Key Largo to Snake Creek

Work was under way in Key Largo throughout the latter half of 1905. Crews hewed their way through the hardwood hammocks, blasted coral rock, and leveled a roadbed in advance of the track-laying teams. They put down track on Key Largo in September of 1906, and Engine 10 arrived by barge on November 14, 1906, before the bridge at Jewfish Creek was finished. It served as a utility locomotive moving supplies and materials on the new track. By January 1907 most of the track on Key Largo was down, ready to carry trains when the bridge was completed.

Fig. 95. Engine No.10 arriving at Key Largo, November 1906. There are also four flatcars on the deck of this barge. It appears that the engineer is ringing the bell. (Jerry Wilkinson)

Fig. 96. Key Largo, Camp No. 2. (Museums at Crane Point Hammock)

The total distance from Jewfish Creek to Tavernier Creek, at the western end of Key Largo, was 18 miles. On February 7, 1907, Henry Flagler took an inspection tour, running from Miami, over the Jewfish Creek Bridge, to the end of Key Largo.

The roadbed was designed to be between seven to ten feet above mean low water throughout the Keys. Since many of the islands are only a couple of feet above mean low tide, the roadbed had to be elevated with fill. This was a laborious process, and several techniques were used at different areas of the Keys.

On Key Largo, the laborers first built wooden trestles as high as the desired level. These trestles were temporary, generally built with the local timber that had been clear cut at the site. A small gauge track was built on top of these trestles, and cars full of sand or rock were hauled along these tracks. The cars were capable of being tipped to either side. When brought to the site where fill was needed, it was dumped from the flatbed car. The workers did this repeatedly until the trestle itself was buried. This technique was especially

useful in marshy areas that did not have a lot of loose rock available.

In order to provide rock for the roadbed, the workers either blasted it from the local right-of-way or broke up rock from quarries and transported it to the fill areas. There was a major rock quarry on Key Largo at 29817+00 (this is where U.S. Highway 1 turns to go up the 18-Mile Stretch today). Drill gangs tamped holes in the coral rock with long steel rods, inserted dynamite, and blasted the rock into useful chunks. They usually loaded the rock by wheelbarrow, but in some cases, they were able to get a steam shovel to do the heavy lifting.

By 1916 Key Largo sported a fully developed station located at 22030+60 (MM 417.25). There were no residences for the F.E.C. employees at this station, but there were two toilets and a water tank. These facilities and the station were on the ocean side of the track. There was also a station on Key Largo at Rock Harbor (MM 424.58, or 22,417+71). The platform and station were on the ocean side. About a thousand feet to the north on the bay side were houses for the sec-

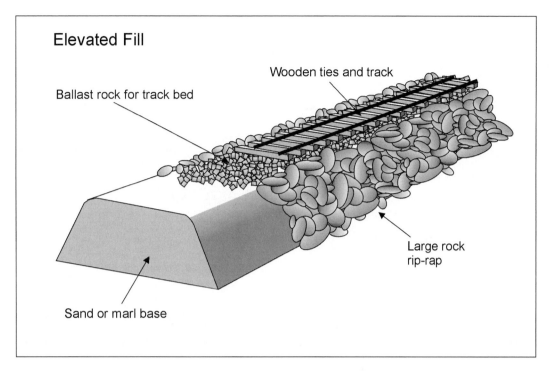

Fig. 97. Building the elevated roadbed with sand and rock.

Fig. 98. Barrow pit on Key Largo. Barrow pits were quarries for rock fill for the roadbed. This pit was located in the area where U.S. Highway One curves to the north below Lake Surprise. (Museums at Crane Point Hammock)

Fig. 99. Drilling gang on Key Largo tamping holes for dynamite blasting. (Museums at Crane Point Hammock)

Fig. 100. Steam Shovel No. 2 at Camp No. 2, Key Largo, is loading blasted rock. (Historical Museum of South Florida)

Fig. 101. Workers dumping rock from temporary trestle. (Museums at Crane Point Hammock)

Fig. 102. Fill is growing. This is the Dove Creek area on Key Largo. (Museums at Crane Point Hammock)

Fig. 103. The finished grade on Key Largo. (Museums at Crane Point Hammock)

tion foreman and a laborer, along with a tool house and a 2,000-gallon water tank.

Tavernier Creek

Building the grade seven to ten feet above the low-tide mark required a lot of labor and material. The engineers tried different methods for doing this at different locations in the Keys. In locations that were close to water and near a source of sand, it was possible to pump fill material to build up the grade. At Tavernier Creek, the waterway that separated Key Largo from Plantation Key, engineers rigged excavators to pump slurry from nearby beds of sand through long pipelines. The pipelines floated on simple pontoon barges, which allowed the excavator some range of movement so it could dig new materials.

The outfall of the pipe was placed on land where the engineers wanted to build up the grade level. The liquid tended to run; to contain the slurry, the workers built fences with flashboard and braced them for the huge weight of the material they were to contain. Evidently it was possible to pump material only a few hundred feet inland.

In 1916 Tavernier had a station located at Mile Post 431. The station platform was at 22752+10. There also were residences for the foreman and laborers at Tavernier, as well as a tool house, all on the ocean side.

Plantation Key

The botany and geology of Plantation Key are very much like Key Largo's. It is a long key and fairly high, but it needed to have the roadbed built up in some areas. Other sections were quite high, and the workers cut rock away to make the grade level. Work crews first hewed a 200-foot-wide swath down Plantation Key for the right-of-way and then began blasting all of the rock they could get from the immediate area. Again,

Fig. 104. The completed grade at the south end of Key Largo taken from a high perspective over Tavernier Creek. This is the approach to the Tavernier Creek Trestle. The whiter fill in the foreground near the bridge is from the pumped-in material. In the distance lies the rock fill. (Historical Museum of South Florida)

Fig. 105. Pipeline on pontoon barges that carried the slurry to the grade site to the north of Tavernier Creek. The outfall of the pipe will go into the wooden containment forms in the distance. (Museums at Crane Point Hammock)

Fig. 106. Wooden forms to contain the slurry for the approach on Plantation Key side of Tavernier Creek. While this may have saved much backbreaking labor for the crews building roadway with rock and sand, it took considerable construction effort to build the containment forms. (Museums at Crane Point Hammock)

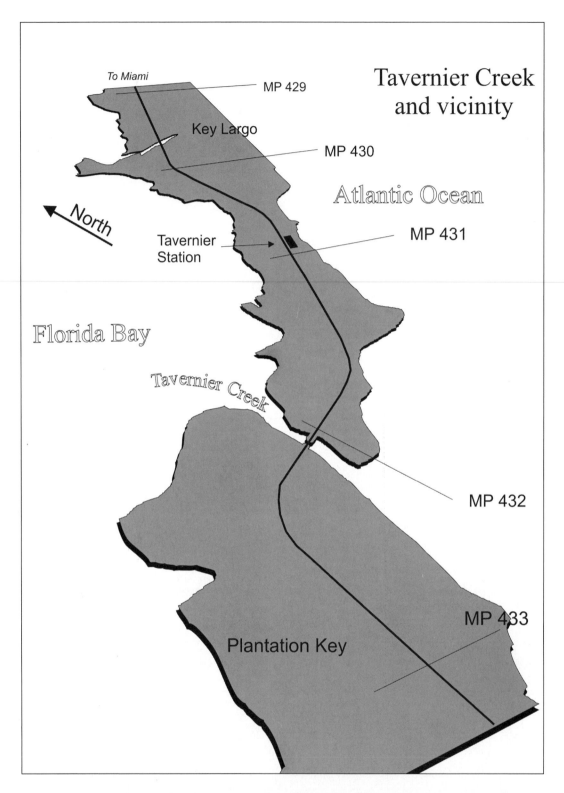

Fig. 107. In this flyover of the Tavernier Creek area we see that the main line took some major curves. The creek itself was not very wide, and the engineers reduced this width further by building approaches from each bank towards the center so that the final trestle was only 32 feet long.

Fig. 108. Completed Tavernier Creek trestle. (Historical Museum of South Florida)

Fig. 109. South end of Plantation Key. Camp No. 11 is in the near distance to the right, the approach to Snake Creek in the far distance. The beginning of the roadbed (to be built with rock) is on the right. The small house on the left is for storing dynamite. (Museums at Crane Point Hammock)

Fig. 110. Quarry on Plantation Key after a blast. Note mule heading out of the picture to the left. Mule power was used at numerous places in the Keys. (Museums at Crane Point Hammock)

they relied on quarries and rock moved from the cuts for the major portion of the fill.

Camp No. 11 was the major camp at Plantation Key. Workers at this site built all of the containment walls for the slurry at the approach at Snake Creek and eventually built the wooden trestle that crossed Snake Creek. The trestle was begun February 14, 1907, and completed by March 12. The bridge had a fixed span and a 25-foot-wide opening, sufficient for the smaller construction work barges to pass through.

Fig. 111. Large chunks of coral rock after dynamiting. A drill gang member appears to be tamping a hole for a second blast. (Museums at Crane Point Hammock)

Fig. 112. Transporting dynamite on barge *Jahncke.* The distinctive sheds warned workers to handle with care. (Museums at Crane Point Hammock)

Fig. 113. Quarry at Plantation Key. Workers are filling the tilt-bed carts. Note the small temporary track for the carts. The carts were built by the Continental Car and Equipment Co. (Museums at Crane Point Hammock)

Fig. 114. A view from the Snake Creek area looking north on Plantation Key. Note again that they were able to fill the approach with pumped-in sand. Camp No. 11 was to the left, but it had been dismantled by the time this photo was taken. (Historical Museum of South Florida)

Fig. 115. View of Snake Creek Trestle looking from Plantation Key to the south. The land in the distance is Windley's Island, now known as Windley Key. (Historical Museum of South Florida)

6

Windley's Island to Long Key

Windley's Island

SNAKE CREEK SEPARATED PLANTATION KEY from the next pair of keys collectively called the Umbrella Keys. These were renamed Windley's Island (sometimes Windley's Islands, and now known as Windley Key) sometime during the construction phase and eventually joined together, first with a trestle, then later with fill. Windley's Island turned out to be a blessing for the project—the coral rock was higher than on any of the other keys. In some places it was as much as 15 feet above sea level. This meant that instead of building up the grade, workers were able to blast rock away that could be used at other sites along the roadbed. Windley's Key became a rich source of rock fill that was used for several years.

Fig. 116. Dredge *Mikado* in Snake Creek. The eastern end of Windley's Island is in the distance. (Museums at Crane Point Hammock)

Fig. 117. Rock fill near Camp No. 8 at Windley's Key. These gentlemen apparently did not have the luxury of tilting carts. (Museums at Crane Point Hammock)

Fig.118. Mule at work at the Rock Cut near Camp No. 8 on Windley's Island. (Museums at Crane Point Hammock)

Fig. 119. Quarrying fill for the roadbed. This photo, dated March 3, 1907, is at Camp No. 8 on Umbrella Key. (Museums at Crane Point Hammock)

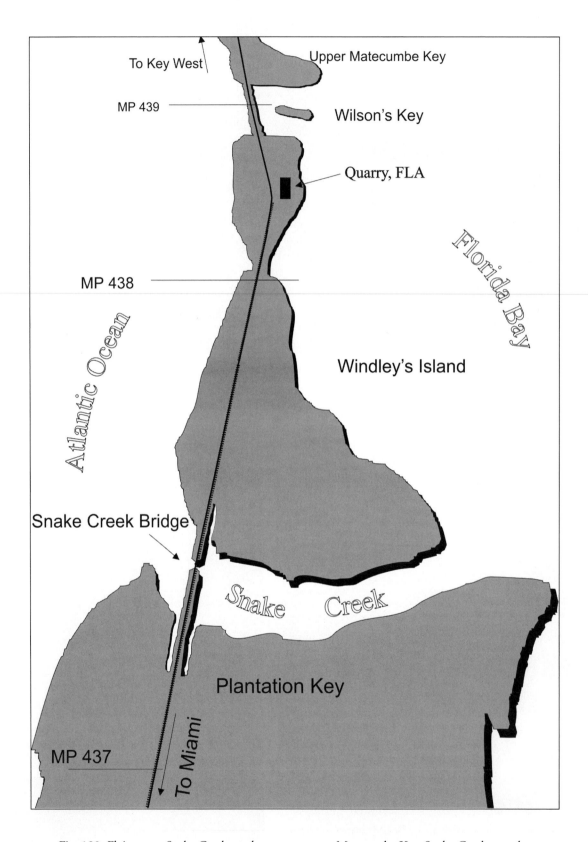

Fig. 120. Flying over Snake Creek on the way to upper Matecumbe Key. Snake Creek was almost blocked with fill; there is just a tiny passageway left at the bridge. The section (Wilson's Channel) between Windley's Island and upper Matecumbe Key was completely filled.

Fig. 121. Camp No. 11 at Windley Key, April 1906. The building with the American flag may have been a post office. (Museums at Crane Point Hammock)

Fig. 122. Inside office, Windley Key Camp No. 8. (Museums at Crane Point Hammock)

A number of rock quarries were established on Windley Key. One major group was on the Florida Bay side at about 23100+00, where the Windley Key Fossil Reef State Geological Site now stands. Another cluster of quarries was located about a mile to the south at 23150+00. One of these quarries is now part of the "Theater of the Sea" complex. In 1916 there was a station named "Quarry" in this area. At the western end of Windley's Island lay another stretch of shallow water that separated the key from upper Matecumbe Key by 2,500 feet. This passage was called Wilson's Channel; a small key named Wilson's Key lay to the north. Workers bridged this gap with a long trestle in August 1907. The trestle was similar to the one installed at Snake Creek, with a 25-foot-wide horizontal passageway for work barges. There was no drawspan for the Wilson Channel trestle. At some time before 1916 this gap was filled with rock and the trestle disappeared.

Fig. 123. Office force in tent in Camp No. 4 on upper Matecumbe Key. (Museums at Crane Point Hammock)

Upper Matecumbe Key

Work began on upper Matecumbe Key in early 1905 with clearing operations. In a similar fashion to the work on Key Largo and Plantation Key, upper Matecumbe needed a lot of fill to bring the roadbed up to grade level.

Islamorada sprang up on upper Matecumbe Key because a number of the F.E.C. upper management decided that they liked the area. William Krome purchased property there in 1907. He platted this in 22 lots, named the streets, and gave the community the name of Islamorada. This area is across from the post office today. In 1916 there was a cluster of F.E.C. structures at 23250+11 (MP 440.3), including tool houses, a laborer's house, and a kitchen. The buildings were on both sides of the track.

Fig. 124. In the dining tent, upper Matecumbe Key. (Museums at Crane Point Hammock)

The Big Water Jump—Upper Matecumbe through Lower Matecumbe to Long Key

The next 10.2 miles from the western end of upper Matecumbe Key to the easternmost end of Long Key was mostly water, broken only by lower Matecumbe Key, 3.8 miles long. By the end of the project, causeways and viaducts covered the remaining 6.4 miles.

Fig. 125. Beginning the fill with sand on upper Matecumbe. This is obviously a low area—all of the stumps are red mangroves. (Museums at Crane Point Hammock)

Fig. 126. The engineers established a barrow pit on upper Matecumbe for rock to stabilize the sand fill. Note the design of the wheelbarrow in the foreground. (Museums at Crane Point Hammock)

Fig. 127. Workers building the elevated fill one wheelbarrow at a time on upper Matecumbe Key. (Museums at Crane Point Hammock)

Fig. 128. Covering sand fill with rock on upper Matecumbe. Photograph is dated April 20, 1906. (Museums at Crane Point Hammock)

Fig. 129. Beginning the crossing, Dredge *Rough Rider* preparing to fill between upper Matecumbe and lower Matecumbe. (Museums at Crane Point Hammock)

While preparing the roadbed on lower Matecumbe Key, the engineers tried a new technique that promised to be faster and less labor-intensive than the techniques used on the upper Keys. They took the utilitarian excavators off the barges that had been their base, put wheels on them, and used them ashore (see Fig. 24 in Chapter 2). The excavators built the roadbed from the materials available on each side. They rode on a temporary track that was put in place and then moved as the work progressed. After trying this work on lower Matecumbe, the engineers determined that, while this technique may have shown promise, it was no faster or cheaper than using laborers and mules, and they stopped using excavators in this fashion.

The distance between upper Matecumbe Key and lower Matecumbe Key was 11,585 feet, or 2.2 miles. Between them lay Tea Table Key and Indian Key. The water was shallow over the entire distance, but there were strong currents

both north and south whenever the tides rose and fell. The engineers pondered the best way to cross this gap, realizing that whatever they did would require a lot of fill because of the great distance.

The very best method for building the causeway would have been to bring in hundreds of barges filled with heavy rock and then dump the rock on the bottom until it was high enough to completely block the channel. From this rock base they could have then put up temporary trestles and added more rock to the causeway. However, with the water so shallow, it would have been impossible to bring in heavily laden barges to the site. When they calculated the amount of barges and rock they would need for the initial pile, they determined that this method was not cost effective.

The engineers then settled on moving large quantities of sea floor materials with hydraulic dredges, which were floating pumps that sucked up material from the bottom, transported it in a slurry mixture with seawater, and deposited it wherever the pipe ended. In theory this was a good method for moving large quantities of material and was a traditional technique used elsewhere in the world. It had worked well at Tavernier Creek for pumping sand for the approaches.

But this method was not well suited for many other places in the Keys. At each water crossing the engineers had to devise the best method to build the fill. They had to evaluate the water depth, the current strength, and the availability and suitability of the fill they were going to use. Thus at sites where the sea floor was sand, they were able to use hydraulic dredges to suck up the bottom and transport it in long pipes to the point of deposit. Sand was a good material because it was easy work for a hydraulic dredge and was a suitable material for building a roadbed on land. However, because it is "light," it was impossible to use for causeway work where there were currents. As soon as the sand slurry was delivered, it was washed away.

More substantial underwater materials such as marl could not be pumped in the same fashion. The engineers devised a method of forcing marl through the pipes. Excavators scraped up the marl and dropped it into hoppers. They then closed the hoppers and used steam to force the material through the pipe to the dump area. While marl worked better than sand, the delivery was slow and the process was abandoned except for a few areas where it worked.

Since it was easy to pump sand and light materials, the engineers attempted to eliminate the currents that washed the deposits away by building wooden bulkheads and containment areas to attempt to stop the water flow. Obviously this kind of filling took much time to

set up. First, great rows of pilings had to be pounded into place by pile drivers. Then wet workers hammered bulkhead boards (termed flashboarding) into place. "It was a web-footed operation all the way," claimed one engineer. In places they installed four bulkheads—two inner ones to catch the pumped marl and two outer ones to catch slurry that escaped from the inner ones. As with the pump/filling operations used at Tavernier Creek, the dredge crews towed miles of large-diameter pipe on floats to the scene, attached them together, and prepared to pump sand from the bay bottom near the shore. The dredges scooped up the bottom materials and dumped them into a hopper that emptied into the pipe. A steam-powered pump pushed seawater through the floating pipe that carried the slurry to the dumping area where the causeway was being filled.

The engineers initially estimated that this mixture would take about a year to harden. However, they were delighted to learn that it solidified within a couple of months because of the highly calcareous nature of the marl. After a year it was so hard that dynamite was required to remove it.

Central Supply

By April 1907 the trestles at Snake Creek, Umbrella Creek, and Tavernier Creek were in place. Wilson's Key Trestle opened in mid-May. Workers now had track down through all of upper Matecumbe Key. The F.E.C. established another major supply beachhead in the Matecumbe area in June 1907. They named this depot Central Supply, and it became the major transfer station for materials bound for the Long Key Viaduct project. Central Supply was built entirely on fill; it was a "wide spot" on the

Fig. 130. Major bulkheading in place near Tea Table. These bulkheads formed a containment area for the slurry of sand and water that was pumped in by dredges *Babcock* and *Rough Rider*. The causeway fill on the left is beginning to dry out. (Museums at Crane Point Hammock)

Fig. 131. The long pipeline carrying slurry to the Tea Table fill. Photo is taken from atop the dredge *Rough Rider* looking back towards Tea Table. (Museums at Crane Point Hammock)

Fig. 132. Dredge *Rough Rider* working on fill between upper and lower Matecumbe. *Rough Rider* was operating as a suction dredge at this time. Photo is dated June 21, 1906. In December 1907 the vessel was rebuilt as a dipper dredge for work lower in the Keys. The island in the distance to the left appears to be Indian Key. (Museums at Crane Point Hammock)

Indian Key fill causeway connecting upper Matecumbe with lower Matecumbe between MP 443 and 444.

By August 1907 regular steamer passenger service commenced from Central Supply and Key West. The *Princess Issena* left Key West on Monday at 7:00 A.M., stopping at excavator camps along the way. It arrived at Central Supply on Tuesday at 11:00 A.M. At 1:00 P.M. on the same day, the boat left for the return trip, arriving in Key West on Wednesday night. A similarly scheduled trip left Key West on Thursday, returning Saturday night. Cost for the excursion was $1.50 per person; meals were 35 cents.

Camp No. 5 was the central housing site for the workers on lower Matecumbe Key. Like the other F.E.C. camps, it had a commissary and dormitory buildings, and it was a reasonably comfortable permanent camp until after the Long Key Viaduct was completed at the end of 1908.

Fig. 133. Central Supply under construction. Bulkheads determined the shape of the land created when the excavators pumped in sand. (Historical Museum of South Florida)

Fig. 134. The station at Central Supply is visible on the left. There is a train with water tanks on the track. (Todd Tinkham)

Fig. 135. Central Supply. Upper Matecumbe is in the distance. Three cars are on a siding to the main line. They can be directly unloaded onto the barge in the foreground. (Monroe County Public Library)

Fig. 136. First train into Central Supply, June 1907. In the distance is upper Matecumbe Key. The wooden bulkheads that contained the fill are visible in front of the platform tents. (Monroe County Public Library)

Fig. 137. Commissary at lower Matecumbe Camp No. 5. Commissaries stocked most of the items the men needed for their personal use. The F.E.C. granted concessionaires permission to operate in the camps. (Museums at Crane Point Hammock)

Fig. 138. Engineers at Camp No. 5 on lower Matecumbe Key. (Museums at Crane Point Hammock)

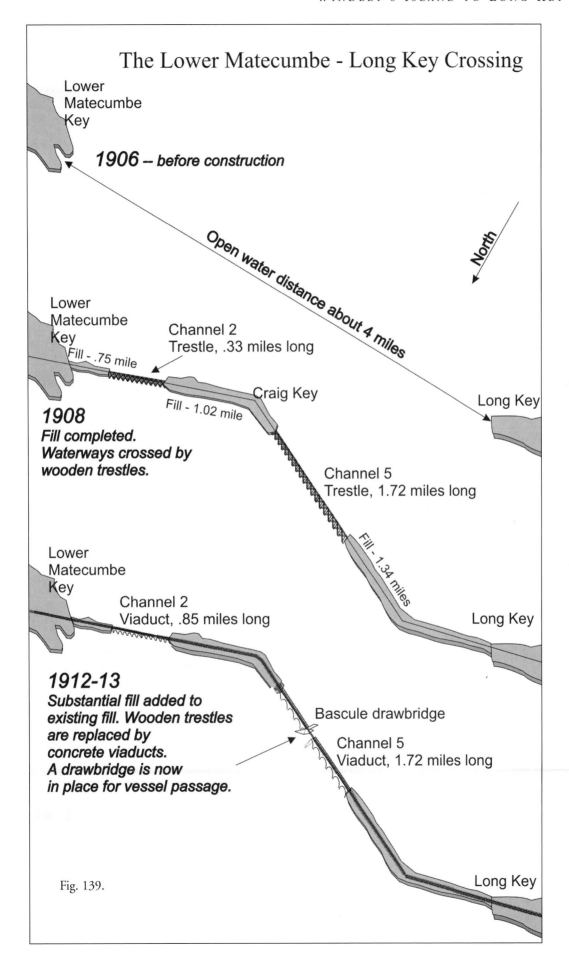

The Lower Matecumbe - Long Key Crossing

Lower Matecumbe Key

1906 -- before construction

Open water distance about 4 miles

North

Lower Matecumbe Key

Channel 2 Trestle, .33 miles long

Fill - .75 mile

Craig Key

Fill - 1.02 mile

Long Key

1908
Fill completed. Waterways crossed by wooden trestles.

Channel 5 Trestle, 1.72 miles long

Fill - 1.34 miles

Lower Matecumbe Key

Channel 2 Viaduct, .85 miles long

Long Key

1912-13
Substantial fill added to existing fill. Wooden trestles are replaced by concrete viaducts. A drawbridge is now in place for vessel passage.

Bascule drawbridge

Channel 5 Viaduct, 1.72 miles long

Fig. 139.

Long Key

Fig. 140. Looking to the east on fill between lower Matecumbe–Long Key crossing. It was later named Craig Key. (Todd Tinkham)

Lower Matecumbe to Long Key

The crossing from lower Matecumbe Key to Long Key was the second-longest water crossing of the entire project, stretching over nearly four miles of open water. Again, the water was shallow, exceptionally so in the middle section. The plan was to build as much as possible with elevated causeways, using fill techniques as was done with the upper-lower Matecumbe crossing. In addition, the engineers knew that they could not confine the water completely. Some passageways were needed to allow the tides to interchange. And there was some concern (later to be proven correct) that filled causeways would be prone to washout by waves and storm surge from hurricanes. Thus the plan for the lower Matecumbe–Long Key crossing included two viaducts. The first at Channel 2 was .33 miles long; the second at Channel 5 was 1.72 miles long. Initially (see Fig. 139) the water gaps were covered by wooden trestles; these were in place by 1908. Later they were replaced with concrete viaducts.

The workers again pumped in sand to create

an island between Channel 2 and Channel 5. Later known as Craig Key (named for a store-keeper who lived there), this island was elevated fill from the surrounding bay bottom. When it was initially completed, the elbow-shaped piece of land looked stark and white as the material baked in the sun.

There was a single leaf bascule drawbridge near the center of the Channel 5 Viaduct. This was a small bridge, the span section only 57 feet long. Unlike the swinging spans used at Jewfish, Indian Key, and Moser, this span was raised by hoisting it up in the air.

There was also a 100-foot drawbridge near Indian Key called the Indian Key Draw. This bridge was removed and filled in August 1912. It was reportedly difficult to operate and often needed repair. It is likely that it was installed for the convenience of the construction fleet and was removed when it was no longer needed.

Fig. 141. Channel No. 5 drawbridge in the up position.
(Albert Perez)

Long Key and the
Great Viaduct

7

Initial groundwork on Long Key began in late 1905 with general clearing operations. Long Key was made considerably longer on its eastern end with the causeway coming from the Channel 5 Viaduct. This key, like the others, had some high ground, but still required a lot of fill to bring the grade up to an acceptable height. Again, the ground was dynamited for fill, workers and excavators scrabbled it into a roadbed, and the land was made ready for track by October 1907.

Some of the land on the western part of Long Key had earlier been cleared for coconut groves. The grand plan called for a hotel and fishing camp at Long Key; this work began as the track was completed to that point. There was also a large work camp at the western end of the island, and 800 men were stationed there during the construction of the Long Key Viaduct. By 1907 few of them were in quarterboats; most were housed on the ground. According to one of the cooks, "the cooking fires never went out." The cooks served 70,000 meals in the month of October 1907.

The Long Key Viaduct

Construction Division engineers were eager to begin the Long Key Viaduct because it would be the greatest test of their skills to date. It was to be a massive bridge, all of poured concrete with steel reinforcing. The bridge was the prototype of three other bridges planned for the Extension and was the model used for many of the other smaller bridges.

The distance between Long Key and Conch Key was 2.7 miles. The water was fairly deep for most of this length, and the currents were strong when the tide ran. Thus the gap could not be filled as a causeway, and it was necessary to build a great viaduct to cross the distance. In the original plan, the engineers wanted to build a short causeway from Long Key towards Conch Key, then a great spandrel arch bridge with 180 arches that would extend 1.98 miles across the deep portion. At this point workers would build a causeway for the remaining distance to Conch Key, about a half-mile away. In fact (see Fig. 144), the 180 tall arches were built, but the planners later found that they could not make

Fig. 142. Camp No. 9 at Long Key. (Museums at Crane Point Hammock)

Fig. 143. Engineers
at Camp No. 9 on
Long Key. (Museums
at Crane Point
Hammock)

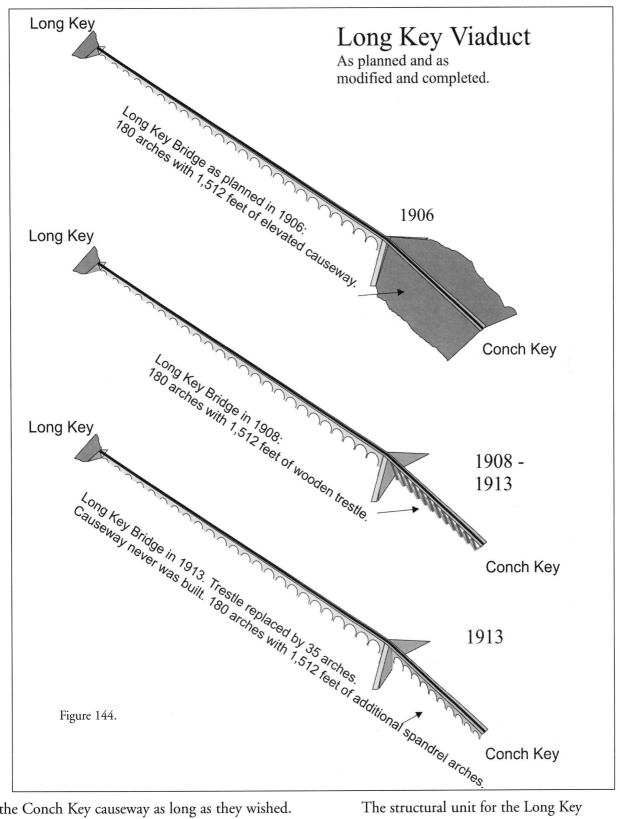

Long Key

Long Key Viaduct
As planned and as
modified and completed.

Long Key Bridge as planned in 1906:
180 arches with 1,512 feet of elevated causeway.

1906

Conch Key

Long Key

Long Key Bridge in 1908:
180 arches with 1,512 feet of wooden trestle.

1908 - 1913

Conch Key

Long Key

Long Key Bridge in 1913. Trestle replaced by 35 arches.
Causeway never was built. 180 arches with 1,512 feet of additional spandrel arches.

1913

Conch Key

Figure 144.

the Conch Key causeway as long as they wished. In 1913 they finally built an additional 35 arches at the west end to join the filled causeway coming from Conch Key.

The structural unit for the Long Key Viaduct (and many more viaducts to be built later) was the spandrel arch. Each arch was to be 50 feet long and raise the track level to 30 feet

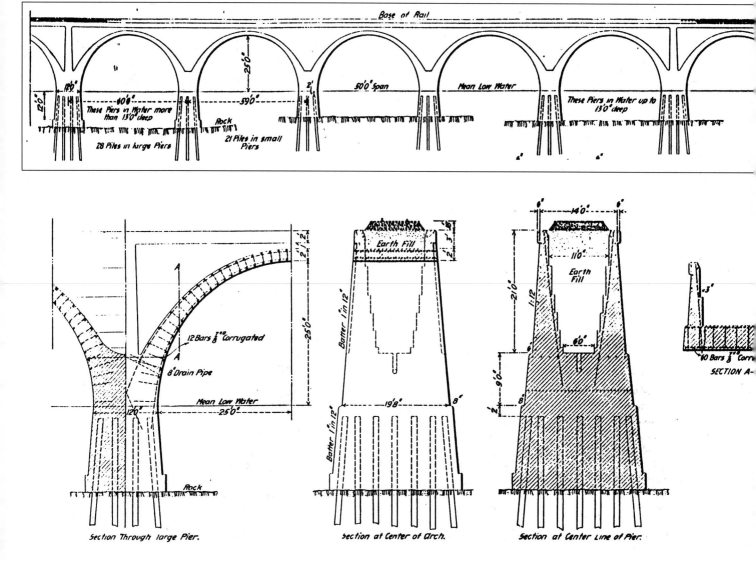

Fig. 145. Elevations and cross sections of the Long Key Viaduct. The upper elevation shows a string of spandrel arches. Note that the leftmost and rightmost piers are thicker than the others. The Long Key Viaduct was built with every fifth pier stronger than the other four, and with additional pilings set in the coral bedrock. In the cross section plans, note that the spans were "hollow" inside, later filled with earth and ballast rock.

above mean low water.

Building these arched spans was a complicated and tedious process. First, surveyors plotted the precise location for each arch. They did this by building a series of survey platforms about 200 feet to the ocean side of the planned bridge; these platforms were a few hundred feet apart. From these fixed stations, the surveyors directed the placement of initial wooden pilings in the general area where the piers were to be built.

The bottom of Florida Bay is limestone, left over from a 100,000-year-old coral reef, and is an excellent base for bridge construction. It is fairly level but in most areas is covered by sand and marine sediment. Thus the workers first had to clean off the area where a pier was to be located. They used excavators and water pumped down under pressure. When they had cleared the

Fig. 146. Small cofferdam lowered in place by derrick. (Monroe County Public Library)

so in diameter, and the wood was green. They placed the pilings in a preset pattern: 28 pilings for the large piers, 21 for the smaller piers. At this time they also put in a number of other pilings to be used later for attaching rigging materials and for supporting other forms.

After the pilings were set, the workers brought in cofferdams. Cofferdams were four-sided boxes with no bottom and were built with panels that could later be disassembled and reused. The height of the cofferdam varied but needed to extend from the limestone bedrock to a couple of feet higher than the water level at the highest tide. The cofferdam was lowered in place over the pilings, then tugged and pushed until it was in the correct location. Workers pulled it down in place with special jacks and secured it so that tides or storms would not move it. The cofferdam was full of seawater. Workmen and divers attempted to make it as watertight as they could at the junction with the bay bottom by placing sandbags all around the outside edge of the cofferdam.

area down to bare rock as well as they could, they drove holes into the limestone with a steel-tipped pile driver. These holes varied in depth; at times the pile driver passed through pockets or caves. After extracting the steel pile, they then inserted wooden pilings and drove them as far as they could. These wooden pilings were a foot or

Fig. 147. Cofferdam in place, anchored by nearby pilings. At this time it is full of water, waiting for the first layer of concrete to be poured in the bottom. (Monroe County Public Library)

Fig. 148. Workman using a simple tremie to send concrete to the bottom of the cofferdam. (Historical Museum of South Florida)

The goal at this point was to pour a solid footing (termed the "seal") underwater. This would serve as a base for the pier to be built and would be a firm connection (along with the wooden pilings) so that the pier would not shift position later. The cofferdam itself became the form for this first pour.

The workers then put the concrete into the cofferdam underwater. This was not a simple task— if they just dumped concrete in, it would be diluted by the water and of no use. They had to "lay" it on the bottom gently. To do this they used a device called a "tremie," a tool not unlike a hose with a funnel at the top. They regulated the placement of the concrete by moving the tremie back and forth in a pattern above the cofferdam, and they kept the funnel full with concrete from a cement mixer barge. When they determined by measurement that there was enough concrete in place (they liked to make the seal about 2 to 4 feet thick), they ended their pouring and removed the tremie. The cofferdam remained in place full of water, and the concrete set underwater.

Fig. 149. A "hole" in the water. Inside the cofferdam the concrete is solid. Workers have dewatered it with the hose. Note the ends of the pilings protruding through— these will help join the next portion of the pier to the seal. (Monroe County Public Library)

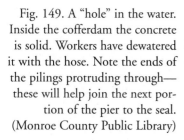

After several days the concrete was solid. The workmen then pumped the water out of the cofferdam. The concrete plug sealed the bottom, and the cofferdam walls kept the seawater out. Workers essentially built a "hole" in the water so that they could begin the next stage. This involved assembling forms inside the cofferdam to shape the "lower section," or the part of the pier that would rise from the seal to above the surface of the water. For most of the Long Key Viaduct, this lower section would be a solid concrete pier about 15 to 20 feet high, 20 feet wide, and 8 to 10 feet thick.

Wooden forms for these piers were built onshore and then brought to the site by barge. The workmen assembled them inside the cofferdam, using steel wire connectors to augment their strength. They placed arrays of steel reinforcing rods deep inside the pier forms that would later help join the lower section to the spans. When all this preparation was complete, they brought a cement-mixing barge alongside the pier forms and dumped buckets of concrete into the lower section form. After this concrete set (and after they tested samples from each batch of concrete), the workmen removed the

Fig. 150. Forms for the lower section of the pier lowered into place inside the empty cofferdam. (Wright Langley Archives)

Fig. 151. Lower section form inside cofferdam. Note the flaring sides of the form. This will meet the curve of the arch form to be brought in next. (Monroe County Public Library)

Fig. 152. Completed lower section of pier showing the reinforcing rod that will be used to connect with the upper section. The forms have been removed, but cofferdam is still in place. (Monroe County Public Library)

Fig. 153. Cofferdam is removed; the stumpy lower section pier is completed and waits for the arch ring forms. (Monroe County Public Library)

forms and the cofferdam. The result was a stumpy pier that protruded a couple of feet above the water; the reinforcing rods made it look like a porcupine. A critical feature of the lower section is an outward flare at the top as it begins the inner curve of the spandrel arch.

Once the lower section piers were in place, the workmen could begin building the spans. The spandrel arches were built with a different set of forms called "arch ring forms" (see Fig. 154), also prefabricated on land. These wooden forms were placed on barges crosswise, towed to the site where they were to be installed, and carefully jockeyed into position so that the ends of the arch ring forms fit between the spreading ears of the lower sections. The engineers planned these form installation trips with the tides in mind, and they used rising tides to lift the barge and arch ring form into place. If they needed to lower the form, they pumped water into the barge to sink it. When the form was in the right place, they blocked it firmly on pilings that were

already driven for that purpose. It should be noted that this way of setting piers and arch forms required a good deal of engineering and construction precision but still allowed for some "sloppy work." The piers could be out of dimensions or placement by a matter of a few inches and still be close enough to be completed.

Now that the arch ring forms were secured, the workers brought in side forms for the spandrel walls. Steam-powered derricks lifted sections of the forms in place. There were 18 panels for each spandrel, which were also prefabricated and quickly secured in place since they matched the arch ring forms perfectly. All of these forms were used several times as the bridge unfolded; 33 sets of forms were used for the 180 arches of the Long Key Viaduct.

One additional set of forms were placed inside the spandrel walls in order to exclude concrete from the interior of the arches. This space was later filled with crushed ballast rock and became the track bed.

Fig. 154. Arch ring form and spandrel wall on land. Early in the project these were built in Miami at the Terminal Docks. Later carpentry shops were established in the Keys for these forms. (Historical Museum of South Florida)

Fig. 155. Three steps of the process. At the left is a barge with an arch ring in position between the flared walls of the piers. The center section shows a ring form blocked in place on pilings driven for that purpose. To the right is a spandrel arch under construction with the side forms assembled. (Seth Bramson)

Although the engineers used steel reinforcing rods in the Long Key Viaduct, the spandrels were designed to be strong enough without the steel. The planners did not have faith that the steel would not rust over time.

The engineers carefully monitored the curing of the concrete. In order to get the maximum strength from the concrete arches, it was important that the forms be released slowly and in a prescribed sequence. The arch rings were unblocked and dropped partially, then completely, in accordance with schedules based on the best science of the time. It should be noted that concrete technology was not in its infancy. The engineers knew a great deal about the performance of this material, and all of them were graduates of good engineering schools.

The Long Key Viaduct concrete work was very much an experiment for the engineers. Previous to this construction, they had built a few abutments with concrete and the pier for the Jewfish Creek Draw, but they were largely inexperienced in viaduct building and made many

mistakes as they learned on the first few piers at the eastern end of the bridge. When divers inspected the piers, they found that there were problems with the concrete being "washed out" from the aggregate because the early tremies were difficult to use and had to be modified. Engineers learned that simply dumping buckets of wet concrete between the spandrel walls did not work well because the reinforcing steel rods and steel braces often blocked concrete from flowing into all areas of the spandrels. According to one report, the initial spandrels were "rough looking work" and had to be patched considerably by masons wherever they found voids. When the concrete was made "wetter" to flow better, much of it leaked out of joints and cracks in the wooden forms. One problem led to another, but the engineers experimented with various mixtures until they were satisfied. By the time they completed the Long Key Viaduct, the construction team was much wiser; this knowledge helped them with the major concrete work ahead of them on the Extension project.

Building the bridge piers

Step 1. Cofferdam forms are set on the bottom. The pilings are punched through the bedrock to hold the completed pier in place. Workers drop sandbags around the cofferdam to reduce concrete leakage and strengthen the cofferdam.

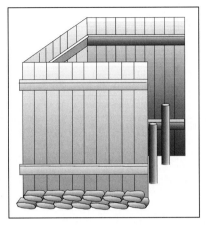

Step 2. Concrete is piped into the cofferdam form to make a seal. When it sets, the pilings will tie the seal to the next level to be poured.

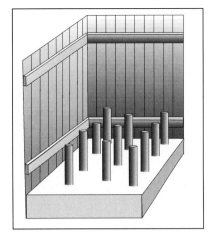

Step 3. Cofferdam is pumped dry. Forms for the lower section are assembled inside the dry cofferdam. The lower section form is now filled with concrete.

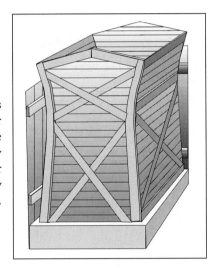

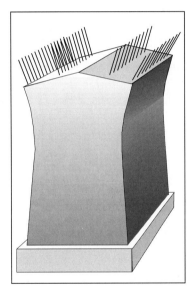

Step 4. Cofferdam and forms are removed. The protruding steel reinforcing rods will tie the lower section to the arch span.

Step 1. Barges bring arch ring forms to the site. The forms fit inside the expanding curve of the lower section forms.

Step 2. Arch ring forms are blocked in place by support pilings.

Step 3. Side forms are attached to the arch ring forms to shape the outside walls of the spandrel arch.

Fig. 156

Fig. 157. High atop the growing bridge, workmen watch as a cement mixer prepares to dump a load of concrete into the spandrel arch wall. (Wright Langley Archives)

Fig. 158. Cement mixer transferring wet concrete from the mixer to the lower section form in the cofferdam. The cement mixing operation went on 24 hours a day—the mixers had electric lights. They were powered by a stationary steam engine. During their busiest times, the mixers could pour one pier per day. (Wright Langley Archives)

The cement mixers were floating factories combining all of the materials at the job site. Each had two derricks. One of them operated the bucket that transferred the wet concrete to the filling forms. The second crane scrabbled sand and rock from barges that brought these materials to the mixer. Engineers monitored the mix and worked to make the pour as continuous as possible so that new concrete always fell in on concrete below that was still wet in order to ensure good bonding. Materials for the Long Key Viaduct came from all over the world. The sand—the basic element for concrete—came from nearby Bear Cut, a barrier island off Miami. The cement itself came from Germany. Early in the project, tests of various concrete samples showed that the German cement was superior to Portland cement for underwater pier construction, and, in spite of the extra expense of transporting this material across the Atlantic, Flagler and Meredith determined to use the best possible product. American cement was used for the above-water spandrel arches. The crushed stone for the aggregate came from the Hudson River, and gravel came from Mobile, Alabama. And finally, an essential ingredient for concrete—fresh water—was not available in the Keys and was brought down by barges from Manatee Creek and other freshwater sources.

Approaches and Abutments

The bridges were always higher than the land level of the Keys. Thus it was necessary to build approaches to the bridges, bringing the grade

TESTING THE CONCRETE

There were no standard tests of concrete until the American Society of Testing Materials established the compression test in 1948 used universally today. The F.E.C. engineers used a simple test to check on the cure rate of the concrete. Each time they poured a batch of concrete, they poured three oddly shaped cement briquettes (or "dog bones" as they are locally known) as test samples of the mortar mix in the concrete. The thinnest part of the test sample measured exactly one square inch. They broke the first of these samples seven days after the pour, the second 14 days after, and broke the third sample 28 days after the original pour. They measured the amount of stress it took to pull the "dogbone" apart. They could then plot these three measurements to determine the cure rate of that batch. This gave them information about the concrete still in forms.

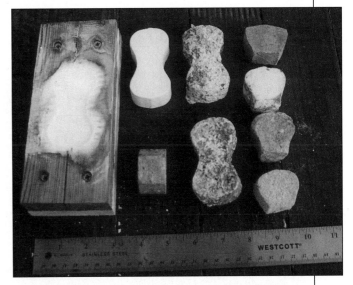

Fig. 159. Concrete briquettes found at Pigeon Key and Knight's Key Dock. The ones on the right are broken, showing that they were tested. The encrusted whole briquettes were found at the Knight's Key Dock area in 20 feet of water. The white one is plaster, made from the mold on the left. The single briquette seen "end-on" just above the 4–5 inch graduations on the ruler shows that the thin portion was precisely one inch wide. Samples courtesy Pigeon Key Foundation Museum. Photo by author.

from the roadbed height to as high as 30 feet for the tallest bridges. The approaches began as far as a half mile from the bridgehead; the construction engineers liked to make the grade very gradual so that the trains would not lose speed as they climbed to the bridge.

Considerable material was moved to build these long approaches. At the Long Key Viaduct, for example, workers first built major wooden trestles for the approach. As with filling at other sites, they used these trestles as a platform for dumping fill. The trestles were much more substantial than the rudimentary ones used for low-level work and were capable of carrying train engines and large dump cars called Goodwin

cars. Filling the approaches took more material than could be moved easily with mules and men.

At the junction where the filling ended and the bridge began, great abutments were built to contain the fill. These abutments were major V-shaped pieces of concrete, rising to 30 feet for the major bridges. They were anchored to the bedrock of the Keys with pilings in the same fashion as were the spandrel piers.

For the Long Key Viaduct, the easternmost abutment began a few hundred feet to the west of the key in the water. There was a second abutment to the west, 180 arches distant. As mentioned, the original plan was to build a causeway from that abutment to Conch Key, but this idea

Fig. 160. View of abutment and approach under construction. The pile driver (center) is setting pilings for the trestle approach; this will rise to the height of the abutment in the foreground. As the pile driver completes a few more feet of the trestle, workers will lay track down so the driver can move forward for the next course. The abutment forms are in an intermediate stage of completion. In the distance lies the filled approach. To the left is a trestle. This may have been a bypass trestle or may have been going to a remote location at a marl or sand pit for the fill. (Monroe County Public Library)

Fig. 161. Abutment forms in place, location unknown. All of the abutments had the same spreading shape. (Monroe County Public Library)

Fig. 162. The great approach trestle rises to the Long Key eastern abutment. This trestle was eventually buried. This photo was taken from Long Key on the ocean side looking to the west. (Jerry Wilkinson)

Fig. 163. In this photograph the viewer is looking to the west and standing on the ocean side of the temporary wooden trestle as it approaches the abutment at the western end of Long Key. Excavator No. 4 is placing material at the edge of the causeway. This trestle will later be buried with marl and rock when hundreds of carloads of fill are brought in to complete the rising approach. (Todd Tinkham)

Fig. 164. The Long Key permanent camp, which was both a housing area and a materials storage area. (Jerry Wilkinson)

was later dropped in favor of 35 additional arches. The original western abutment still stands, acting as a pier. These abutments were termed "wing walls." The engineers built a third abutment for the bridge at the western end when they finally finished the viaduct in 1913.

Long Key developed into a fisherman's paradise when Flagler built the Long Key Fishing Camp. The station was located at 24142+09 (MP 457.2) on the ocean side. Here also were water towers, a pump house, a tool house, an ice chute, and a foreman's residence. On the bay side there was another water tank, a coal bin, and a storage facility.

Clearly, the Long Key Viaduct was a major undertaking for the Construction Division, taking longer to build and costing more than expected. The project taught the engineers much that they put to good use later. It may also have

taught them to avoid building such large bridges out of concrete. The Long Key Viaduct was the only one built with 50-foot arches. Because of its great size and delicate beauty, the Long Key Viaduct became part of the logo for the Key West Extension.

Conch Key to Vaca Key

While construction on the Long Key Viaduct was in progress, other workers were finishing the stretch between Conch Key and Key Vaca. Between these keys lay Grassy Key and a collection of keys called the Crawl Keys.

The Conch Key to Grassy Key crossing was only three miles. The waters were quite shallow for the most part, and the engineers determined to build causeways for most of the distance, with only two short bridges at the Tom's Harbor area. These bridges were wooden trestles when com-

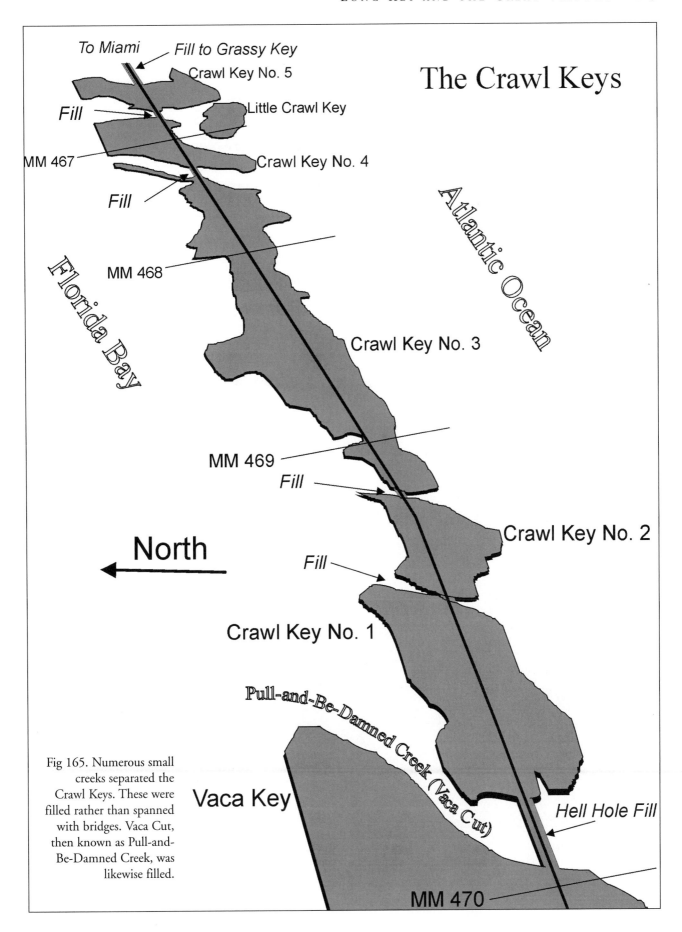

The Crawl Keys

To Miami

Fill to Grassy Key

Crawl Key No. 5

Little Crawl Key

Fill

MM 467

Crawl Key No. 4

Fill

Atlantic Ocean

MM 468

Florida Bay

Crawl Key No. 3

MM 469

Fill

North

Crawl Key No. 2

Fill

Crawl Key No. 1

Pull-and-Be-Damned Creek (Vaca Cut)

Fig 165. Numerous small creeks separated the Crawl Keys. These were filled rather than spanned with bridges. Vaca Cut, then known as Pull-and-Be-Damned Creek, was likewise filled.

Vaca Key

Hell Hole Fill

MM 470

pleted in 1907; arched viaducts replaced the trestles in 1913–14.

The Conch–Grassy causeways in Section 21 required a tremendous amount of fill (mostly marl), and dredges worked for several years from 1907 through 1916, continually adding material to the roadbed. By 1916 the construction crews had placed more than 2.1 million cubic yards of material in this three-mile stretch of the extension, which is about 12 percent of the total fill used for the entire roadway.

Workers on Grassy Key lived at Camp No. 7. Here they continued the traditional sand and rock fill, dynamiting coral rock and gathering it together for the roadbed. The roadbed needed to be elevated six feet above the ground over the length of Grassy Key.

In 1916 Grassy Key had no train station, but there were a couple of F.E.C. houses, two water tanks, and a tool shed located at 22498+38 (MP 426.1), about where the Dolphin Research Center is today.

West of Grassy Key lay the Crawl Keys, a collection of close islands cut by a few small creeks. From west to east, Crawl Key 1 began at Vaca Cut, the other four were consecutively

Fig. 166. Six-foot grade at Camp No. 7, Grassy Key. (Museums at Crane Point Hammock)

numbered as they coursed to the east. Crawl Keys 1–3 were also named Fat Deer Key, and Crawl Key 4 sometimes was called Long Point Key. The engineers and laborers blocked the creeks between these keys with fill as they built the roadbed mostly by hand.

Pull-and-Be-Damned Creek

The water crossing between Crawl Key No. 1 and Key Vaca was named "Pull-and-Be-Damned Creek" on early F.E.C. charts, possibly because of the strong currents that pass through this wide opening between the keys. We can imagine some unlucky man straining at the oars of a rowboat while being badgered by a wife or supervisor shouting "Pull and be damned!" at the hapless oarsman. Whatever its original name, it is now called Vaca Cut and signifies the transition from the lowlands of the Crawl Keys to the relatively higher ground of Key Vaca.

Pull-and-Be-Damned Creek was finally filled and crossed the hard way—by man and mule handling tons and tons of large rock. Although the total distance was only 550 feet,

Fig. 167. Looking to the east from Key Vaca across Pull-and-Be-Damned Creek towards Crawl Key No. 1 as mules and men begin filling the crossing. (Historical Museum of South Florida)

Fig. 168. Hellhole Fill grows across the creek. (Historical Museum of South Florida)

Fig. 169. Camp at Crawl Key. (Todd Tinkham)

the water depth reaches 10 feet in the center, and required a considerable base of large rock. Work began in 1907 and ended in November 1908. Prior to this date, there was no way of crossing the creek with railroad equipment—there was no temporary trestle across this water gap. The workers changed its name to Hell Hole Fill by the time the job was over. This fill was eventually removed in the mid-1950s, and Vaca Cut was spanned by a bridge.

8

The Marathon Construction Complex

CAMP 1 WAS ESTABLISHED on the eastern shoreline of Key Vaca in January 1906. The crews for this section were to prepare roadbed on the eastern end of Key Vaca. Within two months, they moved substantial amounts of material, using the most primitive techniques—dynamite, wheelbarrows, and strong backs—as they worked their way from the east end of Vaca Key towards the middle.

The major development on Key Vaca occurred at the western end of the island, where workers established Camp 10 in 1906. At this time, they were busy with low-level grading tasks as they were elsewhere in the Keys. However, this part of Key Vaca was destined to play a much larger role in the overall plan, and by September 1907, workers cleared land for a

Fig. 170. Workers at Camp 1 at the eastern end of Vaca Key. (Museums at Crane Point Hammock)

117

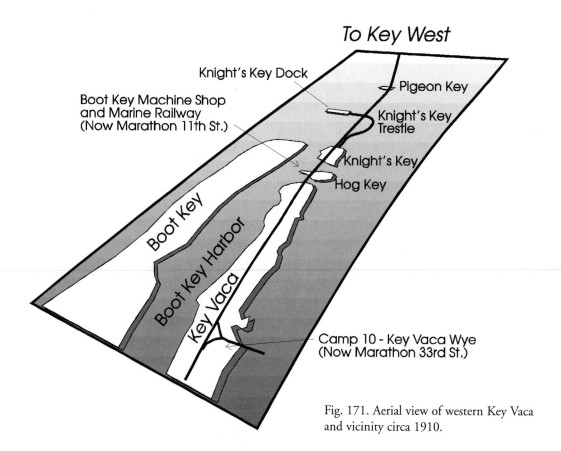

Fig. 171. Aerial view of western Key Vaca
and vicinity circa 1910.

town. This area became the central site for a
major railway terminal and the heart of the Key
West Extension.

If one had been able to take an aerial photograph of the western end of Marathon in 1910,
the picture might well look like Figure 171. The
main line railroad track passes over Key Vaca
towards Pigeon Key on its way to Key West. The
Key Vaca "wye," a large Y-shaped track that
branched off the main line, was located in the
area of what is now 33rd Street in Marathon.
The Key Vaca wye area began as a small camp to
grade and fill the end of the key and then grew
into a small town for the F.E.C. construction
operation. The leftmost block of land is Boot
Key. Boot Key Harbor lies between Boot Key
and Key Vaca, and it was a major staging area for
vessels that moved men and supplies throughout

the Keys. To the west lie little Hog Key and
Knight's Key. Today, the water gaps between Key
Vaca, Hog Key, and Knight's Key are gone; they
were joined by fill when the Extension was built.
Hog Key—now Marathon 11th Street—was the
site of a large machine shop and two major
marine railways built to service the floating fac-
tories and watercraft used to build the Knight's
Key–Little Duck Key Bridge and Bahia Honda
Bridge. Looking farther to the west is the
Knight's Key Dock, first built as a manmade
wooden island, then later connected to Knight's
Key by a trestle. The Knight's Key Dock was initially a supply transfer point, then was converted
to the southernmost rail/steamer terminal in the
U.S. In the distance, tiny Pigeon Key stands as
an isolated island, 2.2 miles west of Knight's
Key. Only five acres in size, this key served most-

ly as a housing area for construction workers and a storage area for cement. All of these units worked together as parts of the Marathon construction complex.

Marathon

This sprawling complex in the middle Keys began in 1906. Most portions were completed by 1908 and were fully operational between 1908 and 1912. At times there were as many as 1,500 men working in the area. The prime goal of the complex was to establish a rail/steamer connection as soon as possible. By opening a temporary terminal at Knight's Key Dock, the F.E.C. could begin commerce and travel to Cuba and other Caribbean ports and start making money.

The next tasks in the middle Keys facilities were to supply and build the great bridges beyond Knight's Key and other projects down the line and to keep the construction machinery operational. From 1906 through 1914, many of the management staff lived at these sites, working shoulder to shoulder, playing together, and sharing family and community life. There was a bold spirit of camaraderie that glued the staff together; indeed, they shared the common goal of completing the grand railway to Key West.

The precursor to Marathon, Camp 10, lay where Switlik School is now located in Marathon, on 33rd Street. Like the other camps, in 1906 it began with a few tents; permanent structures came later. In November 1907, tents were still the major form of housing, but there were a couple of unfinished dormitories, a mess hall, and a few wooden utility buildings.

From the beginning of the project, developing Camp 10 into a railroad junction was a key part of the plan: it was essential to have a major station and rail yard in the middle Keys. Most stations have rail yards right at the terminal. In this case, however, it was not possible since the terminal was a dock nearly a mile offshore at Knight's Key Dock. The wide part of the west

Fig. 172. Workmen, Camp No. 10, Key Vaca, February 1906. This was a temporary camp at the time, and the workers did not have the comfort of tent platforms. (Museums at Crane Point Hammock)

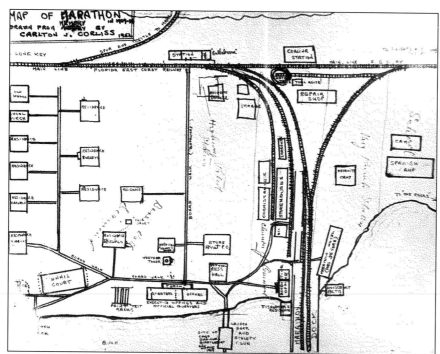

Fig. 173. Hand-drawn map of Marathon, about 1910. The "wye" is on the right. Carlton Corliss provided this map from his recollections in 1952. (Monroe County Public Library)

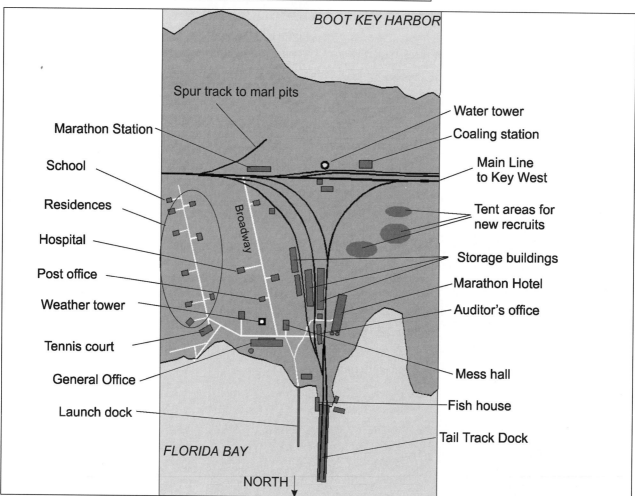

Fig. 174. Corliss' representation can be mapped onto correctly scaled F.E.C. maps, and when done, the true shape of the town is revealed. The Main Line runs from left to right to right as it heads to Key West. The Broadway boardwalk connects the Marathon Station to the General Office. The Tail Track Dock extends northward into Florida Bay.

CARLTON CORLISS AND WILLIAM R. HAWKINS

We know much about Camp 10—and later Marathon—because of the hobbies of two men who chronicled the early town with photos and commentaries. W. R. Hawkins, a draftsman for the F.E.C., took many pictures of the town and endeavored to record almost every building from different angles. He also climbed high atop cranes and other vantage points to shoot panoramic photos. In addition, Hawkins kept a daily journal of the life and times of Marathon. Hawkins' journal provides a running account of the events happening in the small town, including hurricanes, celebrations, and tragedies as well as the day-to-day tennis match scores.

Carlton Corliss also deserves mention as a Marathon historian. He was a clerk in the auditor's office for several years and was also a photographer. Corliss spent a good portion of his later years gathering Marathon memories, published several accounts of the town, and provided a detailed map of the layout of the town. From this map and others, it is possible to locate specifically where the elements of the town lay.

We owe much to Hawkins and Corliss. Thanks to their efforts, we know more about Marathon's role in the Extension construction project than we do about any other part of the Keys.

end of Key Vaca was quite suitable as a substitute rail yard.

Workers began clearing land for the yard in September 1907. They started by preparing an area for the wye. The wye was necessary so that trains could turn around after coming down from Miami. The train would go past the westernmost leg of the wye and stop while the track was switched. The train then backed down the west leg of the wye until the engine was past the junction. Then the junction was switched so that when the train moved forward again, it turned up the eastern section of the wye, heading back to the main line in the opposite direction. This wye lay where 33rd Street now crosses U.S. Highway 1 in Marathon.

The wye was located in this area of Key Vaca because the track arrangement required a lot of land to the north of the main line in order for the trains to be able to have space for the maneuver. As may be seen from old surveys and modern aerial photographs, this was the widest place on the western end of Key Vaca that was

close enough to the Knight's Key Dock. The junction of the wye ended where the Marathon Yacht Club is now. However, this did not provide a long enough "leg" on the wye for big trains, so the F.E.C. continued the track out over the water, about 400 feet beyond the shoreline. This extension became known as the Tail Track Dock.

Workers began constructing the Tail Track Dock in mid-October 1907 and completed it within a month. It had a single track at this time; later the dock was widened to accommodate two tracks. It was more than an extension for the wye; the Tail Track Dock was a main loading area for materials coming to Camp 10, and later served as a supply dock for materials heading to the lower Keys.

Telegraph lines connected the Key Vaca area with Miami on October 26, 1907. The entire roadbed on Key Vaca was completed by this time, and the track-laying work began in early November. The first rails for the wye track were laid on November 2; workers began at the Tail

Fig. 175. Tail Track Dock. Extending 400 feet into Florida Bay to the north, this was a major transfer point for materials during the construction of the Moser Channel Bridge, the Knight's Key Trestle, and the Pigeon Key Bridge. Components of the bridge are stacked on the left of the dock. At the far end of the dock is the generator for the town of Marathon. (Wright Langley Archives)

Track Dock and ran track southeast and southwest to meet the main line, completing the wye in a few days. A barge transported the first train engine to Key Vaca from Long Key, and workers unloaded it at the Tail Track Dock. It was Engine 10, fondly referred to as "Ten Spot," a veteran machine from the work in the upper Keys. A number of construction cars were also ferried to Camp 10; this equipment hastened the track-laying process on the rest of the key. Train whistles first blew on Key Vaca on November 5, 1907.

In early December 1907, there were plenty

Fig. 176. Engine No. 10.
(Todd Tinkham)

Fig. 177. Photo of Marathon from the perspective of the station. Broadway, the boardwalk connecting the station with the General Office, begins at the left and leads to the office in the far right distance. The long buildings are warehouses. The weather tower is also visible in the distance on the right. The building at the base of the weather tower is the hospital. (Curtis Skomp)

Fig. 178. View of Marathon looking towards the Tail Track Dock in the far distance. At the left is the split of the wye. There is an engine in the foreground. The photo was taken from the water tower by the main line. Today one would see this by looking towards the Yacht Club from the perspective of Fishermen's Hospital's parking lot. (Monroe County Public Library)

Fig. 179. The other end of Broadway. This view is looking toward the railroad station in the far distance, with the viewer on the porch of the General Office. The weather tower, hospital and post office are on the left. (Calvin Winter).

Fig. 180. Because of the details that Corliss was able to supply, it is possible to take the older maps and overlay them on modern Marathon. Here we see the main line going along the course of U.S. 1, and see the wye at the 33rd St. area. Also we see how this relates to Fishermen's Hospital at the top, Switlik School, and the boat ramp area of the Marathon Yacht Club today.

of workers on hand in the vicinity of Camp 10, and they rushed to put down the rail between the rail yard and the trestle at Knight's Key. Work proceeded from Camp 10 to the west, over the fill that connected Key Vaca to Hog Key, across Hog Key, and over the fill linking Hog Key with Knight's Key. They reached Knight's Key, about a mile and a half west of Camp 10 on December 10. It is likely that they connected the growing machine shop area at Boot Key Harbor to the main line during this period as well.

On January 22, 1908, trains began running on a regular schedule to Knight's Key Dock. Before this, Camp 10 had been a rough, raw outpost for the workers who cleared Key Vaca, graded the right of way, and put down the steel rail. With an operational railway, Camp 10 became a functional rail yard and material stor-

age depot, operating on a daily basis with a regular schedule. The ragtag construction workers left for sites down the line. In the coming year, the Key Vaca wye evolved into a comfortable, civilized town as it prepared for a bigger role in the Extension construction project.

The Marathon Hotel, owned and built by the F.E.C., was completed in October 1908. It was a grand building with 25 rooms, two floors, and a walk-around upper porch. Overlooking the waters of Florida Bay to the north, the hotel was very close to the Tail Track Dock, and at times it must have been a noisy place to sleep. The first proprietress was Mrs. E.J. DeVore, who lived in a house just south of the hotel. By August 1908, it was reported to be doing a thriving business.

The Marathon area also provided a great amount of material for the construction project.

Fig. 181. General Office for the F.E.C. Key West Extension. Here is where Meredith and later William Krome directed the construction project until its completion in 1916 and beyond. Switlik School is presently located on this site. (Curtis Skomp)

Fig. 182. Marathon Hotel, August 1908. (Wright Langley Archives)

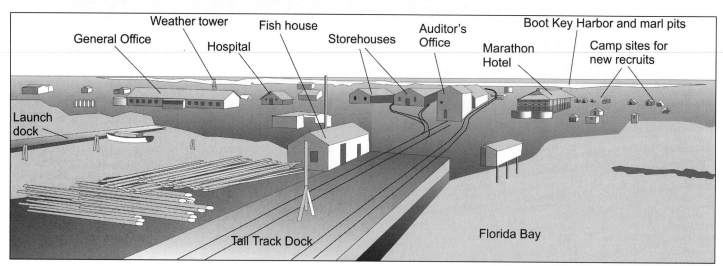

Fig. 183. View of Marathon from the Tail Track Dock. This is a composite photograph from two separate shots taken by W.R. Hawkins as he perched above the Tail Track Dock on a pile driver. Merged by computer techniques, the photos provide a panoramic view of the town. (Monroe County Public Library)

Fig. 184. Tennis was a major sport in Marathon. The gentleman standing on the left is Carlton Corliss. The fourth one from the left standing is W. R. Hawkins. William Krome lived in the house in the background for a period. (Monroe County Public Library)

Fig. 185. Post office in Marathon, 1909. This is the second post office in the town—the first was inside the commissary in 1908. The boardwalk running from left to right in the photograph is Broadway. The main line (not visible) is to the right. (Curtis Skomp)

Surveyors discovered that the bottom of Boot Key Harbor was composed of marl, the best material for building up roadbeds. The workers built two spur tracks on wooden trestles from the main line near the station extending nearly a mile out into Boot Key Harbor. Excavators filled Goodwin cars with this marl from 1910 through 1915 and transferred it to many areas of the Keys. More than 10 percent of the fill for the Extension came from the Boot Key Harbor marl pit.

In 1916, Marathon was still the largest complex maintained by the F.E.C. in the Keys other than the station at Key West. Marathon Station was at 25030+87 (MP 474.06). About 20 of the original buildings were still in use, including residences, warehouses, the commissary, the post office, the kitchen and dining halls, the hotel, and the General Office. The station and the 50,000-gallon water tank were on the ocean side of the main line; the rest of the buildings were on the bay side.

Boot Key Harbor and Hog Key

Boot Key is a large mangrove key on the ocean side of Key Vaca. Between Boot Key and Key Vaca lies Boot Key Harbor, a body of water three miles long and a half mile wide. Most of Boot Key Harbor is shallow. At one point, the F.E.C. considered dredging the harbor to make a port facility instead of building the Knight's Key Dock; this idea was dropped. In January 1908 the dredge *Mikado* scratched out a deep-water entrance to the harbor, while Pile Driver No. 1 drove dolphins for mooring. These preparations provided the shallow-draft vessels access. The workers began building the largest industrial plant ever constructed in the middle Keys—the Boot Key machine shop and boat repair facility. The entire site was termed the Boot Key Harbor and Machine Shop or sometimes referred to as the Boot Key Machine Shop, but no part of it was located on Boot Key. The facility was confined to Hog Key at approximately 25098+00 (MP 475.3).

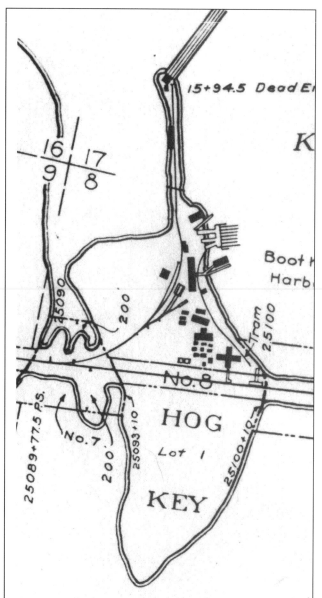

Before the Boot Key Harbor Machine Shop was completed, all damaged equipment and vessels were repaired either in Miami or by a floating machine shop that traveled with the construction project. The F.E.C. needed a major marine repair facility located in the central part of the Keys near the construction effort. The Boot Key site was a perfect location for a permanent repair facility. The shop was within a mile of the Knight's Key–Little Duck Key Bridge and close enough to the Bahia Honda Bridge to be of service to vessels at that location as well. Boot Key afforded the second-best harbor in the Keys, providing a relatively safe place for vessels during hurricanes. And, in the area now known as 11th Street, a spit of land extended southward into the harbor, providing a good site for building marine railways to haul out the vessels for maintenance and repairs.

Fig. 187. The huge machine shop at Hog Key. (Brian Schmitt)

Fig. 188. Boot Key Machine Shop complex. Buildings on the left are dormitories and in the distance lies the machine shop. The photographer is standing on the main line looking due south. (Historical Museum of South Florida)

Fig. 189. This panoramic photo of the Boot Key Machine Shop facility is assembled from two of W.R. Hawkins' photographs. He was apparently shooting from a high tower such as the pile driver in the right foreground. The main rail line goes from left to right in the distance as it heads east towards Marathon, about two miles away (not visible). From left to right are the dining hall (a cross-shaped building), two dormitories (the second dormitory is in the center of the picture), a private residence, and the great machine shop on the far right behind the pile driver. There are a couple of houseboats in the lower left. (Monroe County Public Library)

The first machine shop officially opened at Hog Key on April 13, 1908. W. R. Hawkins, now a resident engineer with the F.E.C., took charge of the facility. The Boot Key complex extended from what is now U.S. Highway 1 about 1,200 feet to the south. A rail spur from the main line ran the full length of the facility (see Fig. 186); several side tracks split from this spur. A second and larger machine shop grew at the site beginning in December 1909. Hawkins was in charge of this construction, though he stepped down as machine shop head before it was completed in 1910.

The great machine shop occupied the central part of the narrow island complex, next to the broad railway. The shop was nearly three stories tall, with lighting provided by high windows. Like many factories at the time, the machines took their power from a central shaft driven by a steam engine outside the building. The shaft spun pulleys that drove the huge lathes, drill presses, milling machines, and other tools in the shop.

The boatyard had two large marine railways extending into the shallow waters of Boot Key Harbor. The southernmost was quite long, jutting out towards the southwest nearly 400 feet. Closer to the mainland lay another set of railways, shorter in length but wider. Both were large enough to carry more than one large vessel at a time. On October 7, 1909, for example, launches *Edna, Hobo, Columbia, Clinker, Curlew* and quarterboats *Delta, No. 1,* and *Miriam* all were under repair at the yard on that day. Workers maneuvered vessels to the railways at high tide and positioned them crosswise on the rails. Large winches pulled them higher, and when the tide ebbed, all parts of the hull and propulsion equipment were easily accessible to workmen. By 1909, there was also a sliding cradle, 72 feet by 100 feet, used to haul the huge cement mixers.

There was a tremendous collection of construction resources at Boot Key Harbor. On April 8, 1908, an F.E.C. inventory of the plant at Boot Key shows 76 vessels floating in the channel between Knight's Key and Hog Key. Eleven additional vessels were described as sunk on the shoals in the area. Most of the floating plant vessels were barges (57 barges, the largest 30 feet by 100 feet and the smallest 9 feet by 25 feet). Other workboats included 5 cement mixers, 3 pile drivers, 2 excavators, a derrick barge, and a few other specialized vessels. Launches *Sadie, Junior, Ida Bell Lounds, Wapiti, Dixie,* and *Lotus* were there, as was steamer *Defiance.* Most of these vessels were anchored in rows, poised for the big task ahead of building the Knight's Key Bridge.

There were a number of permanent residents at the Boot Key yard who occupied a few small buildings and a dormitory or two. There were no families at the yard; all of the staff with families lived in Marathon and commuted.

Within a few yards of the main line was a large cross-shaped building that served as the kitchen and dining hall for the camp. The kitchen was located in the northern end of the cross; seating was in the other ells. There were 150 workers at Boot Key in 1910. A few of these were machinists and mechanics and helpers; it is likely that many of the rest were laborers who worked on the vessels.

Knight's Key Dock

During the period when most of the construction work focused on grading and filling land, an amazing project was growing out at sea. The Knight's Key Dock began as a freestanding platform nearly a mile from Knight's Key and stood in water 20 feet deep, able to service ocean-going steamers. Construction began on the dock in January 1906. In May of that year, the dock sported a derrick for loading and unloading supplies. By June there was enough international shipping arriving at the dock (mostly cement) that a U.S. Customs officer was stationed there. Other heavy materials arrived to be off-loaded; on June 8, 1906, three barges of rock were reported unloaded at the dock for redistribution. By June 15, the dock was 150 feet long and growing. In August, the dock was 600 feet long and 75 feet wide. A few storage buildings were in place. The dock platform was under construction continually until mid-1907.

The dock was not connected to land for more than a year. In April 1906, workers began a temporary trestle from Knight's Key that eventually reached the dock. This was a light-use trestle that was later replaced with a sturdier one for commercial service.

In January 1907, C. S. Coe, a newly hired resident engineer, was in charge of construction at the Knight's Key Dock. Under his leadership

The Knight's Key Trestle and Dock

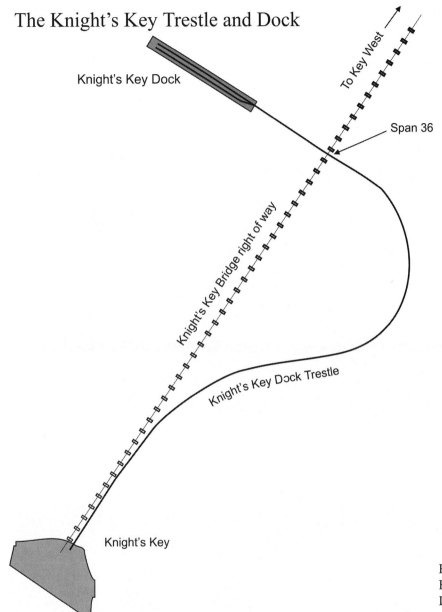

Knight's Key Dock

To Key West

Span 36

Knight's Key Bridge right of way

Knight's Key Dock Trestle

Knight's Key

Fig. 190. Schematic of the Knight's Key Trestle and Dock.

during that year, the dock was enlarged and finally connected to Knight's Key by a permanent trestle. The first piles for the "permanent" Knight's Key trestle were set in October 1907. The trestle was completed and the final rail laid on the day it opened—January 22, 1908.

The Knight's Key trestle looked very much like a question mark. The "bottom" of the question mark touched Knight's Key, then swung north into Florida Bay. It then curved back to the south into deeper water and passed through

the area where the Knight's Key Bridge would soon be built. This trestle appears to have been quite substantial and supported a single track that split into two at the Knight's Key Dock. The question mark shape was planned carefully around the piers of the Knight's Key Bridge— the trestle passed underneath the bridge at Span 36, 2,800 feet from the bridgehead at the west end of Knight's Key.

In January 1908, the buildings and terminal on Knight's Key Dock were not finished, but the

Fig. 191. Knight's Key Dock under construction. The heavy timbers crisscross in the foreground; in the background is a gantry for transferring materials. A pile of crushed stone awaits pickup. Photo is dated October 4, 1906. (Museums at Crane Point Hammock)

Fig. 192. Stockpile of crushed rock on Knight's Key Dock. The dock was continually in use as a transfer point for materials long before it was finished as a terminal. (Museums at Crane Point Hammock)

Fig. 193. Knight's Key Dock, early 1912. This photograph was taken from the Knight's Key Bridge (the track on the right). (Jerry Wilkinson)

dock was pressed into service to receive the first passenger trains from Miami. Rail commerce officially opened on January 22. It took a few more months to put the dock in the form it was to have for the next four years as a major rail/steamer terminal. A hotel boat lay at the dock in January to accommodate passengers of the railroad and the ocean-going steamers. A small hotel built on the dock in March replaced this vessel. By this time, workers also completed a train shed and a quarter house for personnel who worked on the dock. In the central area lay a passenger terminal with food vendors. Some of the earlier equipment was removed; the blacksmith shop was torn down in April. Also in April, the Knight's Key Dock was connected to the mainland by telephone, and, on April 13, 1908, a U.S. Post Office was established at the site. Regular passenger service from Miami to Knight's Key Terminal began on February 5; these trips connected with steamers that cruised to Key West and Havana. Day trips from Miami became popular. In September, tourist excursions came down from Miami to the Knight's Key

Dock for a round trip rate of $2.00.

And so the Knight's Key Dock became the southernmost shipping terminal in the U.S., connecting rail service with ocean-going steamers. As part of the overall plan, the F.E.C. began collecting steamers before the Extension was under construction. During the last years of the nineteenth century, Flagler had moved into the steamship business. He formed the F.E.C. Steamship Company in 1897 and commissioned his first vessel, the S.S. *Miami*, which went into service in 1898. In 1900, the F.E.C. Steamship

Fig. 194. Knight's Key Dock in its heyday as a terminal. The gantry is visible in this photograph. (Jerry Wilkinson)

Company combined assets with the Plant Steamship Company and became the Peninsular and Occidental Steamship Company. Most of these steamers were built for coastal service and were designed to carry freight and passengers. They ranged from 100 to 200 feet in length, and required water depths greater than 15 feet to accommodate their draft. When the Knight's Key Dock was completed, steamers that formerly ran from the Terminal Docks in Miami took up new routes with Knight's Key Dock as their base for excursions. Figure 45 shows the *Montauk*, one of the P&O steamers at Knight's Key Dock.

Pigeon Key

Resident Engineer Coe surveyed tiny Pigeon Key as a construction campsite in July 1908. After sounding the water depth around the island, he notified Krome that it was a good place for a permanent camp, and he supervised building a sturdy dock extending from the east side towards Key Vaca to give workboats access to Pigeon Key in deep water. Shortly afterward, crews of carpenters swarmed over the five-acre island and began building what may have been the most densely populated community in the Keys at the time. Within a few months, Pigeon Key sported three new dormitories, a large mess hall, and a great cement warehouse. A fourth dormitory fol-

lowed; additional housing grew with tent platforms in rows. At peak periods during the bridge-building years, more than 400 men (and a few women) lived on Pigeon Key.

The island was almost in the center of the seven-mile gap where the bridge was to be built (MP 478 is on Pigeon Key). This made it easy to get the workers to the remote construction sites. By virtue of its isolation, the island remained relatively free of mosquitoes and was an easy place to defend from the "booze boats" that continually tried to supply the island-bound workers with the one thing they were not supposed to have.

Most of the workers on Pigeon Key were laborers, but there was a small core of engineers, draftsmen, and skilled tradesmen. Workers bunked in dormitories, 64 men in each building.

Fig. 195. (above) Worker's tents on Pigeon Key. These were on sturdy wooden platforms. In the hurricane of 1909, most of these tents were blown down, but the platforms remained undamaged by the storm. The building in the background is the commissary. (Wright Langley Archives)

Fig. 196. (left) Dormitory building on Pigeon Key. There were four of these, each housing 64 workers. (Monroe County Public Library)

Fig. 197. The commissary at Pigeon Key. Steel deck plates of the Pigeon Key Bridge are visible in the background to the right. Note that this building has buttresses on each side. (Wright Langley Archives)

The dorms had electricity; Pigeon Key, like Marathon, had a generator. Meals were provided by camp cooks and served in a large mess hall on the east side of the island. The kitchen was central to the mess hall complex; this building still stands. Sanitation was simple: there were four outhouses on docks on each corner of Pigeon Key. The island had a bakery, a commissary, and an infirmary tent.

The professional staff on Pigeon Key had some privileges. A few were allowed to build small cottages at the north shore of the island. Coe brought his houseboat *Miriam* to Pigeon Key in 1909 so that his family could be with him during most of the year. Ed Sherran, general foreman for the Seven-Mile Bridge project, lived on Pigeon Key until February 1912, when he moved to Marathon after the first trains were running to Key West. Professional engineers, many of them young and fresh out of college, were often fed and "mothered" by Coe's wife, Lulu. There was some camaraderie between these young engineers, who played croquet for fun on the rocky ground to the north of the cement warehouse. When the tennis court in Marathon was finished in 1910, they managed to get to town to play.

The first tall piers for the portion of the Seven-Mile Bridge that passes over Pigeon Key were finished in the fall of 1909. Steel spans soon followed in December of that year. The bridge towered over tiny Pigeon Key; it still dominates the island today.

Fig. 198. Panoramic view of Pigeon Key, south side of the island. From left to right lie the dining hall/ kitchen complex, then four dormitories, and a field of tents. The two-story building behind the dorms was the construction headquarters shown in Fig. 199. (Jerry Wilkinson)

Fig. 199. Construction headquarters on Pigeon Key. Here C.S. Coe, with his assistant engineers and draftsmen, managed the complex task of building the bridges across the seven-mile water gap. The building sat at the southernmost part of Pigeon Key. Note that the building also has outside buttress bracing—this was not uncommon at the time. (Curtis Skomp)

Fig. 200. Playing croquet on the north side of the cement warehouse. The woman leaning against the building is C.S. Coe's wife, Lulu. Her daughter Miriam is addressing the ball, and Coe's personal assistant N.B. Nickerson is between them. (Wright Langley Archives)

9

Knight's Key to Little Duck Key

THE DISTANCE BETWEEN Knight's Key and Little Duck Key is approximately seven miles. It took the workers four long years to bridge this gap with what we now call the Seven-Mile Bridge. The bridge was never called by this name while the construction project was under way; the name apparently evolved sometime in the 1930s.

During the construction process the crossing was considered as four separate bridges—the Pacet Channel Viaduct, the Moser Channel

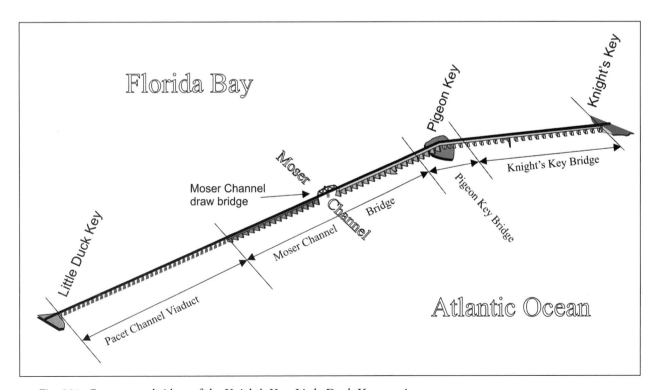

Fig. 201. Component bridges of the Knight's Key–Little Duck Key crossing.

Fig. 202. Most of the crossing was built on tall piers with steel deck plate spans. This photograph of the completed bridge is looking towards Knight's Key. The accessory trestle to the Knight's Key Dock is in the left background. (Monroe County Public Library)

Bridge, the Pigeon Key Bridge, and the Knight's Key Bridge. Sometimes the entire section was called the Knight's Key Bridge. Figure 201 shows the four sections from the west to the east. Beginning at the western end, the Pacet Channel Viaduct comprises 210 spandrel arches, each 35 feet long; they are in very shallow water. The Moser Channel Bridge begins at this point and traverses to within a few hundred feet of Pigeon Key. Over this long distance, the bridge is built with steel deck plates on top of tall piers, except at the drawspan section. The Moser section is quite low at the end of the Pacet Viaduct (about 17 feet from the water to the top of the track level), but it gradually rises to its full height of 30 feet. All of the spans in the Moser Channel Bridge are 80 feet in length and rest on the classic tapered piers that give the bridge its distinctive appearance.

There is a short section of 19 spans that passes over Pigeon Key. These are steel deck plate spans but are only 60 feet long, and, because they carry over a shorter distance, the plates are just 7 feet tall. The shorter spans were necessary to build in the radius of the curve at Pigeon Key. The Pigeon Key sec-

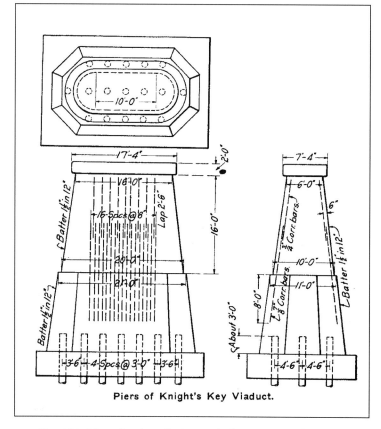

Piers of Knight's Key Viaduct.

Fig. 203. Plans for the tall piers with dimensions. Those in deeper water had a wider seal and broader lower section. Note that they used wooden pilings inside the concrete to keep the seal firmly on the bay bottom. This figure also shows the reinforcing rods inside the pier.

Fig. 204. Tall piers in forms at the Knight's Key end of the bridge. The engineers are standing on the Knight's Key Trestle. (Monroe County Public Library)

Fig. 205. Stately and majestic, a line of the tall piers grows to cover the distance from Knight's Key to Pigeon Key. (Wright Langley Archives)

tion also has different piers—instead of the smooth, tapered piers, the concrete supports on Pigeon Key are square and blocky and appear unfinished.

The Knight's Key Bridge extends from Pigeon Key to Knight's Key. This long span, nearly two miles, repeats the architecture of the Moser Channel Bridge, with tall, tapered piers and 80-foot deck plate sections. The elevation of the Knight's Key Bridge is 26 feet from the track level to the water at the Pigeon Key end, but climbs to 30 feet as it rises to the easternmost

wing wall. It stays this height all the way to the abutment at Knight's Key.

In order to build the tall piers for the deck plate bridges, the engineers took lessons they had learned earlier by building the spandrel arches. Again, they used cofferdams to make a seal for the bottom of the pier, dewatered the sealed cofferdams so that they could build lower sections, and then assembled prefabricated forms to make the upper tapered pier. The lower sections were shaped differently (see Fig. 203), and the piers were more substantial in deeper water.

Fig. 206. Large floating derrick about to hoist a deck plate from a barge. (Monroe County Public Library)

The forms for the tall piers were quite complex, with an artistic taper plus a rounded cap on the upper portion. One wonders why the engineers went to so much trouble to make the piers pleasing to the eye. Certainly no passengers on the trains would ever see them.

When the piers were completed, workmen installed steel spans on top of them. First, they placed steel pedestal plates directly on the concrete. Then they set an 80-foot-long deck plate section on the pedestal plates and bolted them to the pier with eight bolts. This completed half of the span; the other side was similarly swung in place and bolted. At this time steel workers riveted the internal bracing (these pieces came partially assembled) to the two big beams, giving them great strength.

After the deck plates were in place, workers

Fig. 207. The steel deck plates installed on the piers above Pigeon Key at the curve. Marathon is in the far distance. (Monroe County Public Library)

laid the wooden railroad ties crosswise on the steel. The ties were larger than standard, 11 feet long and 10 inches square. At the points where they rested on the steel, the ties were carefully milled to fit the top of the deck plate beams so that they would not shift laterally. Each tie was carefully trimmed by hand so that it fit well and did not "rock" as weight passed over it. The ties were not attached to the steel deck plate but were tied together with major bolster curbs on each side of the track.

Moser Channel is about 20 feet deep and is fairly well centered between Knight's Key and Little Duck Key. Here the engineers built a large

Fig. 208. Lifting ties up to the level of the bridge. A steam-powered crane hoists a load of the heavy ties from Pigeon Key to the span above. (Wright Langley Archives)

Fig. 209. Crew of workers carrying a tie down the Moser Channel Bridge. They are using a device similar to ice tongs connected to the long wooden handle. (Wright Langley Archives)

Fig. 210. Workers trimming the ties so that they fit tightly to the steel deck plates. In this photograph Pigeon Key is in the distance. Note that the worker in the middle has no shoes, and is walking on the creosoted ties with bare feet. (Wright Langley Archives)

swing-span drawbridge for vessels. Termed the Moser Channel Draw, this large structure was built on site in the "open" position. The steel components were manufactured by the American Bridge Company of New York, brought down to the Boot Key Machine Shop area by train, and carried out by barge as required.

Workers began by building a great cofferdam in the center. Inside this they assembled forms for a round pier that rose 40 feet; this pier was solid concrete and measured nearly 25 feet in diameter. The drawbridge was started on July 1, 1909, and completed on January 31, 1911.

The Moser Channel Draw was powered by

a gasoline engine, and the mechanic who assembled the rotation mechanisms, R. T. Kyle, became the first bridge tender (see Fig. 79). He and his family lived on Pigeon Key, and he held the position until his death in 1926.

As with the Long Key Viaduct, the Knight's Key Bridge began with a large abutment at the eastern end to contain the great amount of fill that would be put in for the approach to the bridge. To build the abutment, workers drove pilings for the outline of the shape for their forms and more pilings in the middle so that the abutment would have no tendency to move or tip with the weight of the earth that it would

Fig. 211. The huge cofferdam surrounds the lower section forms for the Moser Channel Draw pier. (Monroe County Public Library)

Fig. 212. Assembling additional forms for the rising pier at the Moser Channel draw. (Monroe County Public Library)

Fig. 213. Completed Moser Channel Draw in the "closed" position. Trains went through the truss bridge. The bridge rotated 90° to a position parallel to the trestles seen below the bridge. This trestle was used to support the bridge while it was under construction, and left in place after completion. (Monroe County Public Library)

Fig. 214. Initial forms for the abutment at Knight's Key, eastern end of Knight's Key Bridge. The excavator in the central portion appears to be adding to the fill that will rise to the 30-foot level of the abutment. (Monroe County Public Library)

Fig. 215. Setting the steel deck plates at the Knight's Key abutment. The engineers first attempted to place the deck plates using a huge crane mounted on a train car. They installed the spans and the crossbeam stiffeners, put on the ties, then laid track so that the crane could advance 80 feet toward Key West. They then repeated the operation for the next span. The subcontractor doing this work gave up the job after the 1909 hurricane, and the F.E.C. Construction Division took over, using barges to set the deck plates. (Monroe County Public Library)

THE EXTENSION AS A HAZARD TO NAVIGATION

Not everyone was delighted with the concept of a railway over the Keys. Local fishermen and commuters in particular complained that the viaducts and causeways blocked their passage between the Keys. They were forced to go many miles out of their way to access a drawbridge if they were on one side and needed to get to the other. The U.S. Naval Command at Key West made an issue of the blockage of their open water access from their headquarters.

A snippet from the *Key West Citizen*, July 17, 1907, reads: "Masters of coastal smacks and vessels are pronounced in their expressions that the best harbors of refuge are being obstructed by viaducts and bridges in such a manner that it will be impossible for vessels encountering

rough weather and seeking refuge to get in or out of same."

To respond to these criticisms (and to enable the engineers to move their own supply and construction craft as necessary) five drawbridges were built into the Extension: Jewfish Creek Draw, Indian Key Draw, Channel 5 Draw, Moser Channel Draw, and a small draw at Key West where the fill approached Trumbo Point. The Indian Key Draw was removed before 1916. There is no doubt that the Extension seriously impeded navigation in the Keys, especially since most of the vessels of the time were sailboats with masts too tall to go under any of the viaducts.

Fig. 216. Beginning the wooden trestle at Span No. 36. The Knight's Key Trestle is the curved track going between the piers of the Knight's Key Bridge. (Wright Langley Archives)

Fig. 217. Temporary trestle at Span 36 is finished. This photo is taken from the Knight's Key Dock looking northward towards the Knight's Key Bridge. The train coming to Knight's Key Dock sneaks under the Knight's Key Trestle at Span 36. (Historical Museum of South Florida)

Fig. 218. The Pacet Channel Viaduct under construction. These spandrel arches were built in the same fashion as the Long Key Viaduct. (Curtis Skomp)

eventually contain. The Knight's Key abutment rose 30 feet above the water.

The engineers chose to cross Pacet Channel with spandrel arches. These arches were smaller than those used for the Long Key Bridge; each span covered 35 feet, for a total distance of 7,350 feet, or 1.4 miles. The arches did not have reinforcing steel inside, and because they were smaller, they were much easier to build than those at the Long Key site. However, considering that there were 210 arches, each with cofferdams, lower sections, and arch rings to be built, the Pacet Channel Viaduct required substantial work. It was begun in August 1910 and finished in November 1911.

Carpenters camped at the Pacet Channel

end to build the cofferdams and arch ring forms. While many of the forms could be used repeatedly, some were damaged as they were taken down and were rebuilt as necessary.

While the Knight's Key Bridge was completed in September 1910, it was not fully finished in its final form. Span 36—the span that passed over the Knight's Key Trestle—was intentionally not set in place on the piers. The gap was bridged instead with a wooden trestle, which allowed the bridge to be used without the final steel span. If the steel span had been used, trains would not have been able to get out to Knight's Key Dock. It was essential to have this dock open until the railway was completed to Key West since it was a major passenger terminal.

WHY TWO TYPES OF BRIDGE?

Engineers design bridges so that their spans will be higher than the largest possible wave that nature can generate in her wildest storm. Wave height is related to water depth. Deeper water generates higher waves and therefore requires a higher bridge to ensure that the waves will not carry the structure away. Higher bridges require more concrete as well as more expense, especially if they are built with spandrel arches.

The engineers thus determined to use the spandrel arch style for the shallower areas of the Keys such as the Pacet Channel. Where deeper water required higher bridges for the Knight's Key crossing, they built with the cheaper steel deck plate style bridge rather than use the huge 50-foot spandrel arches that had cost so much to build at the Long Key Viaduct. The steel deck plate bridge also required many fewer piers than the spandrel bridge for the same distance.

10

Bahia Honda and the Lower Keys

BETWEEN THE END of the Pacet Channel Viaduct and Bahia Honda Key lay several small keys—Little Duck Key, Missouri Key, and Ohio Key. Reportedly some workmen named these latter two keys after their home states. The gaps between these keys were bridged with trestles by 1910; the trestles were replaced with spandrel arches in 1914.

The Missouri–Ohio Viaduct was begun in February and completed in April. Workers then moved to the Little Duck–Missouri span from April until June, and finally completed the Ohio–Bahia Honda section in August 1914.

West of these keys lay a cluster of low keys collectively called Bahia Honda Key. Early work in 1905 and 1906 completed a long, filled causeway through the shallow center of Bahia Honda. At the westernmost tip of Bahia Honda lay the

Fig. 219. Camp at Ohio Key, 1911. This unknown quarterboat served as housing for the workers. The aft section, low to the water, housed the toilet and shower. (Monroe County Public Library)

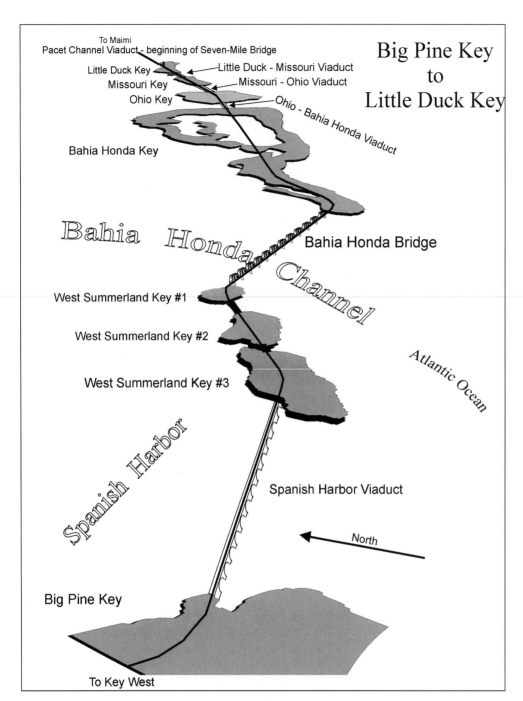

To Maimi
Pacet Channel Viaduct - beginning of Seven-Mile Bridge
Little Duck - Missouri Viaduct
Little Duck Key
Missouri - Ohio Viaduct
Missouri Key
Ohio Key
Ohio - Bahia Honda Viaduct

Big Pine Key
to
Little Duck Key

Bahia Honda Key

Bahia Honda Channel

Bahia Honda Bridge

West Summerland Key #1

West Summerland Key #2

West Summerland Key #3

Atlantic Ocean

Spanish Harbor

Spanish Harbor Viaduct

North

Big Pine Key

To Key West

Fig. 220. Flyover view of Bahia Honda and nearby keys. While we think of Bahia Honda as a "solid" key, the center of it is actually a lagoon with a causeway passing through it.

greatest engineering challenge facing the Extension project—Bahia Honda Channel.

The Bahia Honda crossing was a problem because of strong currents and deep water. The engineers were not sure how to approach it and did not commit to a final plan until 1907, long after the rest of the Extension was under construction. They toyed with the idea of siting the

crossing more to the north, where the water was shallower and currents weaker. One newspaper claimed that the train would end at one side of Bahia Honda, then use a ferry to cross. In 1906 an article from the *Florida Times Union* noted that the plan was to span the distance with 60-foot steel deck plates. There was even speculation that Bahia Honda could become the end of the line; it had a deep harbor, and there was no need to go to Key West with the track. No solution to bridging Bahia Honda Channel would be easy or cheap.

The planners could have chosen to build a bridge like the Knight's Key steel bridge, but building piers for that kind of bridge was a problem. Because of the great water depth (30+ feet in the center), engineers had to use steel cofferdams for the seal; wooden forms could not withstand water pressure at that depth. This made it difficult and expensive to build piers that tall. Over the distance of nearly one mile, they would have needed a total of 64 piers to support 80-foot steel deck plates, and some of the piers would have reached more than 50 feet. In order to decrease the number of piers, the engineers decided to make the spans longer, a feat they could do only by building a truss bridge.

There were many truss railway bridges in the U.S. by this time, and the engineers knew how to build them. They decided to place these trusses on tall piers like those used for the Moser Channel Bridge. Then they went to work optimizing the design for the piers and trusses.

The final bridge was built with steel through-truss sections (the train went through the truss). Thirteen spans were 128.5 long, 13 spans were 186 feet, one span in the center was 247.5 feet, and at the western end of the bridge, they finished with nine deck plate spans of 80 feet each. This truss bridge required only 34 piers, a considerable savings compared with a complete deck plate bridge.

The truss components were prefabricated and brought to Bahia Honda by barge. There was a steel dock on the ocean side of Bahia Honda, which became the transfer point for the materials. They were stored in a great holding yard until needed. The heavy pieces were brought to the work site by train flatcars.

The main Bahia Honda camp was located on a small, low island at the very tip of the beginning of the crossing (see Fig. 225). There appear to have been four or five buildings and a number of platform tents on the bay side of the

Fig. 221. Completed Bahia Honda Bridge from a postcard. (Monroe County Public Library)

right-of-way, and one large building on the ocean side.

There was also a work camp located a little to the east of the great curve of the eastern approach. Known as the Bahia Honda Sand Pit Camp, it was occupied from 1909 to 1911. Considerable sand was taken from this pit and distributed at the Bahia Honda construction site as well as up and down the line.

Before any steel was set on the bridge, the workers first built an abutment and an approach trestle for flatcars bringing the components for the bridge. This rising wooden trestle began about a third of a mile to the east of the abutment and climbed to the 30-foot height. The trestle bridged a waterway that separated the Bahia Honda camp island from another part of Bahia Honda. The approach was completed in February 1911.

There was considerable modification to the shape of Bahia Honda as the project progressed. In 1907 the first camp occupied the Florida Bay side of a small key along the right-of-way (see Fig. 208). This camp was later dwarfed by the large wooden trestle that brought the approach to the bridge from ground level to the eventual height of 30 feet at the abutment. By 1911 dredges pumped thousands of cubic yards of fill, first closing the gap between the camp island and mainland Bahia Honda. They continued this filling, using marl and sand delivered by Goodwin cars until they built the great embankment and buried the original trestle.

As with all the other bridges, the workers first tackled the abutments that defined each end of the bridge. They built a mighty abutment that rose 21 feet above mean low water. The first stages included driving pilings and building great forms in the shallow waters at the western end of

Bahia Honda and the eastern end of West Summerland Key 1. They were simultaneously working on the tall piers for the bridge; this process was identical to that used for the Knight's Key and Moser Channel bridges, except that the lower sections were in deeper water.

The trusses were assembled in place on top of the piers. To do this, the workers first had to build a wooden structure (termed "falsework") beneath the area of the steel to support the beams while they were being assembled. They drove pilings all along the route and built a wooden bridge so that they could assemble the steel bridge on top of it. Part of this wooden bridge supported a track on each side of the steel

Fig. 222. A train engineer's view through the trusses on Bahia Honda Bridge. (Todd Tinkham)

Fig. 223. Bahia Honda Sand Pit Camp was located at 25582+00. (Jerry Wilkinson)

Fig. 224. Eastern abutment at Bahia Honda. The photographer is shooting to the east from a derrick located near the third tall pier for the Bahia Honda Bridge. Forms for two tall piers are nearing completion, as are the forms for the eastern abutment. On the left lies the camp, and the steel dock is on the right in the center of the photo. The wooden trestle for the approach appears to be taking shape, curving from the center of the abutment to the left. (Curtis Skomp)

Fig. 225. Standing on the abutment at Bahia Honda camp looking to the east. The camp is on the left. Note that the wooden trestle crosses a water passage between the camp and a larger island in the distance. To the left of the trestle in the water lie a string of pilings; these will later be used to hold fill as the trestle is buried. Photo date is prior to 1910—the filling has not begun. (Jerry Wilkinson)

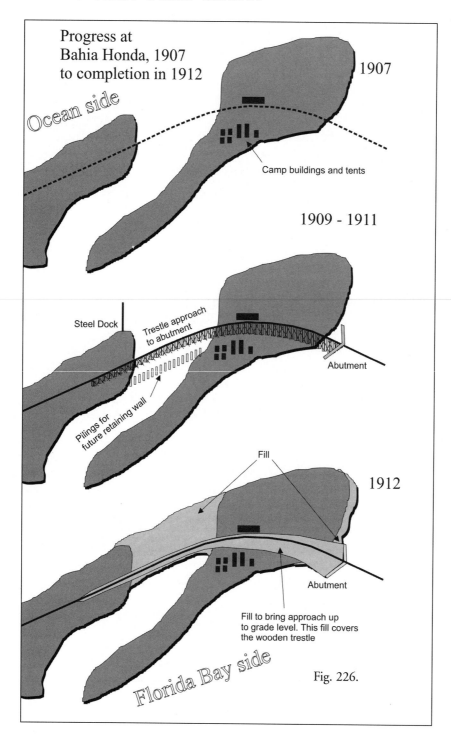

Progress at
Bahia Honda, 1907
to completion in 1912

Ocean side

1907

Camp buildings and tents

1909 - 1911

Steel Dock

Trestle approach
to abutment

Abutment

Pilings for
future retaining wall

Fill

1912

Abutment

Fill to bring approach up
to grade level. This fill covers
the wooden trestle

Florida Bay side

Fig. 226.

bridge; these tracks were for a gigantic gantry called a "traveler." The traveler was a rolling wooden crane device that was used as a scaffold for the men to climb and to lift the steel parts into place for assembly.

Unlike the scattered construction of the bridges connecting Knight's Key with Little Duck Key, the Bahia Honda Bridge was built in a linear fashion. Workers began building the first truss in January 1909, starting at the eastern end of the bridge near the camp. The eastern end of the truss rested on the east abutment. Then slowly but surely, they completed one truss, moved the traveler west, and then built the next truss. The workers stopped on October 9, 1909, because of a hurricane and did not resume until March 1, 1910.

Fig. 227. The traveler was a rolling scaffolding that was moved to the span construction site as necessary. (Todd Tinkham)

Fig. 228. Two of the trusses are complete; a third is in progress inside the traveler. Note that the embankment for the approach to the eastern abutment is finished. Also note that the pilings for the falsework are in place on the right side of the photograph. Date of this photo is early 1909. (Jerry Wilkinson)

By July 22, 1910, fourteen piers were finished. Twenty-one were completed by February 8, 1911. Eight 128-foot trusses were completed on July 5, 1911; by August 6, nine of the 128-foot and two of the 186-foot trusses were finished, with a twelfth well under way. During that month, the workers finished three spans. There were 300 workers at Bahia Honda during this period. The entire bridge was completed in January 1912.

Work continued at Bahia Honda long after the Extension was operating. Dredge operators continually pumped in additional marl to build up the approaches on both the east and west ends. In 1914, a set of 18-inch-thick concrete retaining walls were built on the west side of the bridge; these walls extended from the abutment down the length of the West Summerland Keys.

Spanish Harbor

At the west end of West Summerland Key lay the crossing to Big Pine Key at Spanish Harbor. This crossing was not very deep and was bridged

Fig. 230. Bahia Honda camp after the bridge is finished. All that remains is a material handling track and a single building. (Monroe County Public Library)

originally with a wooden trestle. After the Extension opened in 1912, workers began building a spandrel arch viaduct for the permanent track. Work began in April 1912 and was completed on October 18 of that year. The total distance of the crossing was about 5,000 feet. Workers filled an approach from West Summerland Key towards Big Pine Key for part of this distance, and from Big Pine Key eastward for a short distance. The viaduct itself covered 3,312 feet when completed. These arches were medi-

um-sized, with 35 feet between piers.

Most of the remaining spandrel bridges in the Keys today do not look like the original viaducts because the Overseas Highway conversion added a deck 22 feet wide over the original bridges. In many places this "new" deck has railings as well. At Spanish Harbor the highway deck was removed (cut off on both sides) to match the width of the original viaduct. Today the Spanish Harbor Viaduct looks most like the original spandrel bridges. Two spandrel sections

Fig. 231. A look inside the spandrel walls at the east end of the Spanish Harbor Viaduct, 1998. The inner space was filled with ballast rock when it was completed. (Photo by author.)

Fig. 232. Train on trestle. A trestle such as this had an expected service life of 10 years. It was thus important that they be replaced with more durable spandrel arch bridges, which had a much longer period of maintenance-free service. (Steele)

were removed from the Spanish Harbor Viaduct, and it is possible to see the inner structure of the spandrel arch.

Big Pine Key

The largest railway construction on Big Pine Key other than the roadbed itself was a fresh water collection center in the middle of the island. Big Pine Key was able to supply some of the water needs for Extension construction. The geological structure of the lower Keys is such that limited fresh water is available in strata close to the surface; a thin layer (or lens) of fresh water lies above the salt water that is found beneath all of the Keys. In July 1906, workmen completed a 100,000-gallon tank on Big Pine. By January 1907, engineers stripped this surface and created a fresh water pond on Big Pine, and they built tanks and trenches to manage the water and fill the huge tank. The reservoir was 90 feet long, 40 feet wide, 15 feet deep, and it was said to hold one million gallons. While this seems like a large quantity of fresh water, it varied seasonally and was only enough to supplement the great

Fig. 233. Footings for the huge water tank on Big Pine Key. Note that there are real pine trees; Big Pine Key and several of the lower Keys have a landscape quite different from that of the upper Keys. (Museums at Crane Point Hammock)

Fig. 234. (left) Track on Big Pine Key near MP 492 and water tank. (Jerry Wilkinson)

amounts needed for the project. It was not nearly enough for the thirsty steam boilers.

Big Pine Key in 1916 had a post office at 25967+80 (MP 491.8). About 300 feet to the south lay a cluster of working buildings, including tool houses, a kitchen, toilets, and three water tanks. On the bay side were platforms and the section foreman's house.

Big Pine Key to Cudjoe Key

Cudjoe Key lay a short seven miles from the end of Big Pine. Between Big Pine and Cudjoe lay Torch Key, Ramrod Key, and Summerland Key. The largest water gap was at Pine Channel, separating Big Pine from Torch Key. Here the engineers determined that they could build an island causeway for

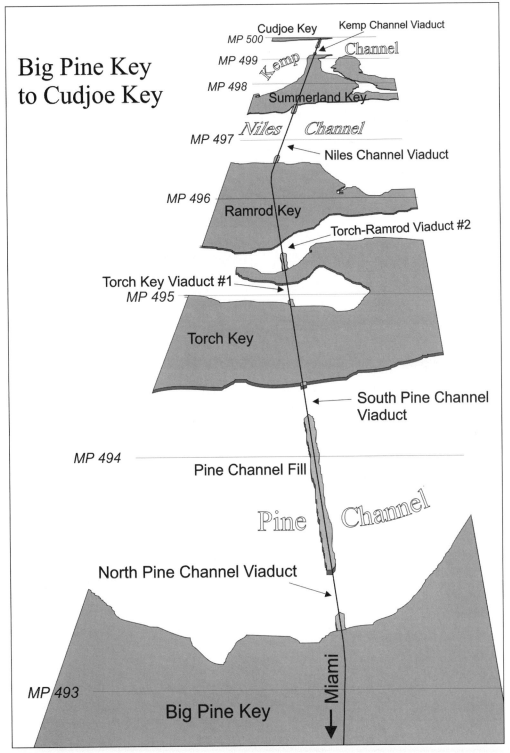

Big Pine Key
to Cudjoe Key

Cudjoe Key
MP 500
Kemp Channel Viaduct

MP 499
Kemp
Channel

MP 498
Summerland Key

Niles Channel
MP 497
Niles Channel Viaduct

MP 496
Ramrod Key

Torch-Ramrod Viaduct #2

Torch Key Viaduct #1
MP 495

Torch Key

South Pine Channel
Viaduct

MP 494
Pine Channel Fill

Pine Channel

North Pine Channel Viaduct

Miami

MP 493
Big Pine Key

Fig. 235. Looking towards Key West from Big Pine Key, there are several major water passages between Big Pine Key and Cudjoe Key. Each of these was first bridged with wooden trestles, then later with spandrel arches.

much of the crossing, and, as they did with the lower Matecumbe–Long Key area, made a new key for their convenience and named it Pine Channel Fill. They then connected this island to Big Pine with the North Pine Channel Viaduct; the South Pine Channel Viaduct connected Torch Key with the Pine Channel Fill. Both of these concrete viaducts were completed by October 1911 and were in place for the inauguration of service to Key West.

This area was far from the main incoming material depots—Marathon, Bahia Honda, and

Fig. 236. Camp at Big Torch Key. Note that, in order to get enough material for the roadbed, they dredged canals (middle of photo). These canals also served as "hurricane holes" for the floating barges and work craft. (Todd Tinkham)

Fig. 237. Camp No. 82, Ramrod Key. The camp at Ramrod appears to be on the eastern shore of the key. The dock/walkway in the foreground may have connected Ramrod with the causeway under construction at the west end of Torch Key. (Museums at Crane Point Hammock)

Fig. 238. Ramrod Key roadbed looking to the east. (Museums at Crane Point Hammock)

Fig. 239. Camp at Niles Channel, July 22, 1909. Ramrod Key is in the distance.(Jerry Wilkinson)

Fig. 240. From the size of the forms for the spandrel arches and the long distance to land, this photo is possibly from the construction of the Niles Channel Viaduct. (Steele)

Key West. For this reason it is suspected that the workers in the camps at Big Torch Key, Ramrod Key, and Summerland Key felt exceedingly isolated. The camps established here were rudimentary, with few buildings. Most of the housing was in tents.

The Torch Key–Ramrod Key connection required two water crossings. Both of them were wooden trestles until concrete arch viaducts were completed in February 1915.

West of Ramrod Key lay the formidable Niles Channel. Possibly because of the current and depth, it was not feasible to cover much of the distance with a causeway, so the engineers built the longest bridge in the lower Keys at this site—2,435 feet, or just short of a half-mile long. This was bridged with trestles in 1911 and later converted to spandrel arches. The Niles Channel Viaduct was begun in March 1915 and completed in November of that year. It was the last bridge finished on the F.E.C. Extension.

Fig. 241. Off to work on Summerland Key. Apparently qualifications for employment included a good sense of balance. (Museums at Crane Point Hammock)

Fig. 242. Caption on the back of this photograph reads, "Water Boys, Summerland Key, Camp 81" and is dated February 6, 1906. (Museums at Crane Point Hammock)

Fig. 243. Beginning the roadbed at Cudjoe Key, February 1906. (Museums at Crane Point Hammock)

Fig. 244. Looking across Kemp Channel towards Summerland Key from Cudjoe Key. The Kemp Channel Viaduct is in the center of the picture. Smoke in the sky over Summerland Key indicates that a train is on the main line. (Louis "Pete" Bow)

Summerland Key

Camp 81 was at Summerland Key. Photos of the period suggest that this remote camp was a difficult place in which to live and to work. Materials for fill were not close by, and much of the roadbed was built in standing water. Crews of workers brought rock and fill from the nearby areas by wheelbarrow on plank walkways.

Cudjoe Key

Kemp Channel separated Summerland Key from Cudjoe Key. It was deemed suitable to do most of this crossing with causeways running from the keys towards the center of the channel. The short (993 feet) space of open water was bridged by a wooden trestle until the final spandrel arch bridge was finished in March 1915.

In 1916 Cudjoe did not have a station, but at 26393+13 (MP 499.8) there was an F.E.C. house and toilet, a pump house, and a 50,000-gallon water tank. See Figures 35 and 36 for photos of this cluster of buildings.

Sugarloaf Key

The camp at the western end of Sugarloaf was called Dr. Harris Camp. Dr. J. V. Harris owned

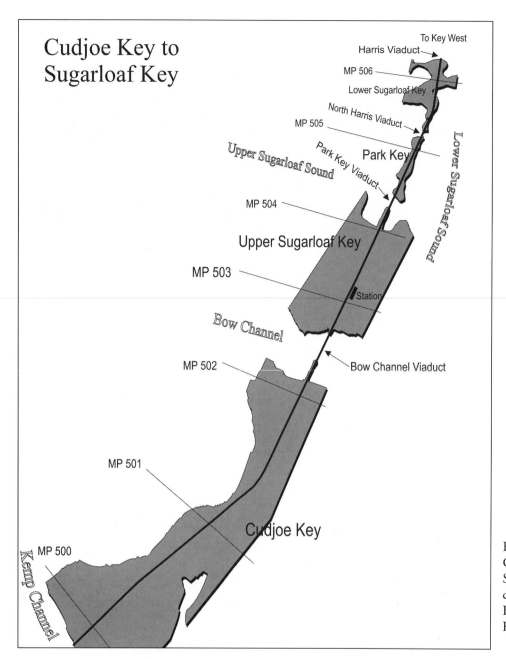

Cudjoe Key to Sugarloaf Key

To Key West

Harris Viaduct

MP 506

Lower Sugarloaf Key

North Harris Viaduct

MP 505

Park Key Viaduct

Park Key

Upper Sugarloaf Sound

Lower Sugarloaf Sound

MP 504

Upper Sugarloaf Key

MP 503

Station

Bow Channel

Bow Channel Viaduct

MP 502

MP 501

Cudjoe Key

MP 500

Kemp Channel

Fig. 245. Flyover from Cudjoe Key to Lower Sugarloaf Key. The major channels to cross were at Bow Channel and Park Key.

Fig. 246. Dr. Harris Camp on Sugarloaf Key. (Jerry Wilkinson)

Fig. 247. The excavator is digging rock and sand from the shallow bottom and placing it on the developing causeway at Lower Sugarloaf Sound. Workers are re-handling the material to get it in the right place. (Jerry Wilkinson)

the property; he sold it to Charles W. Chase, who later renamed the property "Chase." During the construction period, Harris leased or sold land to the F.E.C. for the camp. It is probable that the camp was in the area of Mile Post 506. The viaduct at the western end of Sugarloaf was called the Harris Viaduct; the small opening at the eastern end of Sugarloaf is called Harris Gap, and the viaduct connecting Park Key with Lower Sugarloaf is the North Harris Viaduct. The railroad station (completed by 1916) lay in the area of 26568+00 (MP 503.1). At this site were three water tanks, a residence for the section foreman, two toilets, a kitchen, and a tool house, all located on the bay side of the track.

The Saddle Bunch Keys

Within the last 15 miles to Key West lay a cluster of keys named the Saddle Bunches. The easternmost began just west of Lower Sugarloaf Key, and the group extended about five miles to the west.

Because the Saddle Bunch Keys are in a very low-lying area, they required a great amount of fill. Records show that workers placed almost 1.3 million cubic yards of rock and marl in this section. Because all of the water

Fig. 248. Excavator on barge working at Sugarloaf Sound. The excavator is digging a canal for the barge and using the material to build the roadbed. (Jerry Wilkinson)

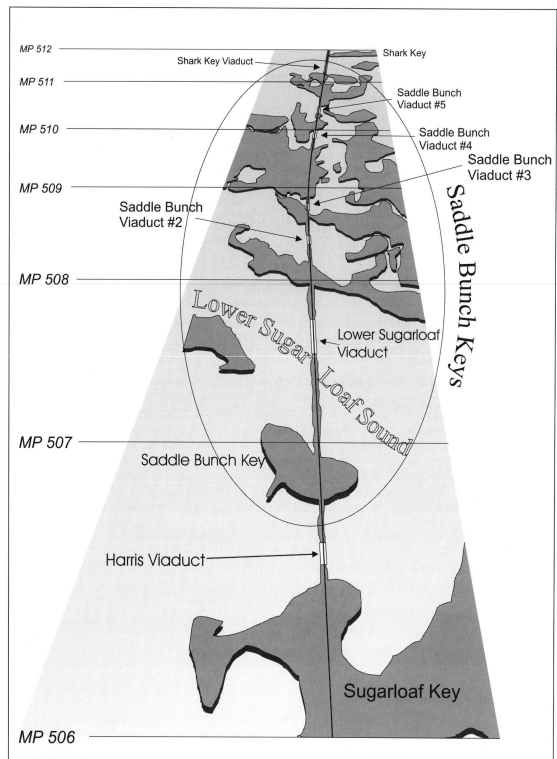

MP 512

Shark Key Viaduct

Shark Key

MP 511

Saddle Bunch
Viaduct #5

MP 510

Saddle Bunch
Viaduct #4

Saddle Bunch
Viaduct #3

MP 509

Saddle Bunch
Viaduct #2

MP 508

Lower Sugar Loaf Sound

Saddle Bunch Keys

Lower Sugarloaf
Viaduct

MP 507

Saddle Bunch Key

Harris Viaduct

MP 506

Sugarloaf Key

Fig. 249. Flyover of the Saddle Bunch Keys. While there were many places that required crossing over water, all of these were quite shallow and easily bridged with causeways. The engineers soon replaced them with concrete viaducts because they were concerned about washouts from hurricane storm surge.

crossings were very shallow, it seems likely that they were initially bridged with rock fill instead of wooden trestles. However, the engineers knew that fill would be washed out in major storms and hastened to put spandrel viaducts through the Saddle Bunch Keys at an early date. Starting in June 1911, they built the spandrel viaduct at Rockland in two months. Then they sequentially built Saddle Bunch Viaducts 5, 4, 3, and 2; this last one was completed in December 1911. These viaducts were short and relatively low, only 12 feet above the water. Initially they were

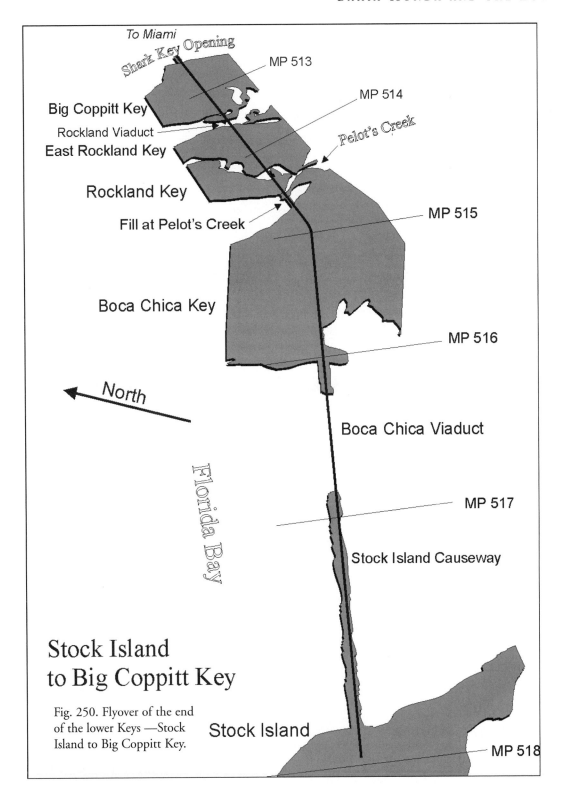

To Miami

Shark Key Opening

MP 513

MP 514

Pelot's Creek

Big Coppitt Key

Rockland Viaduct

East Rockland Key

Rockland Key

MP 515

Fill at Pelot's Creek

Boca Chica Key

MP 516

North

Boca Chica Viaduct

Florida Bay

MP 517

Stock Island Causeway

Stock Island
to Big Coppitt Key

Fig. 250. Flyover of the end
of the lower Keys —Stock
Island to Big Coppitt Key.

Stock Island

MP 518

built with no abutments; these were added on a couple of years later.

Big Coppitt Key to Stock Island

The last big jump before Key West was the stretch between the Shark Key Opening and Stock Island. Here lay from north to south (see Fig. 234) Big Coppitt Key, East Rockland Key, Rockland Key, and Boca Chica Key. A short viaduct installed at the Big Coppitt–East

Fig. 251. Excavator No. 4 at Big Coppitt Key. (Museums at Crane Point Hammock)

Rockland junction was completed in August 1911. Pelot's Creek separated Rockland Key from Boca Chica Key; this was filled in completely.

The camp at Big Coppitt Key was opened in May 1906. There was no station at Big Coppitt, but the F.E.C. built a dormitory, a water tank, and a house for the section foreman at 27042+48 (MP 512.2).

The major crossing that remained was the link from Boca Chica to Stock Island. The total distance between the keys was about 1.7 miles. Here the water was not very deep, and most of this distance was covered by causeway. Begun in 1905, this causeway was completed in February

Fig. 252. This photo was taken August 3, 1907, from a derrick or other tall piece of equipment looking east from Big Coppitt Key. In the middle distance would be the south end of Shark Key; in the far distance lie the Saddle Bunch Keys. Although the right-of-way is cleared, there is no sign of the roadbed grade in place. (Jerry Wilkinson)

Fig. 253. Grade with track on Boca Chica Key.
(Monroe County Public Library)

1906 as a solid land bridge between the islands.

After the Hurricane of 1909, the engineers surveyed the damage to causeways up and down the Keys and determined that they needed to put in more bridges than they initially planned. The causeway between Boca Chica and Stock Island was one of the sites. Thus, in April 1910, they began building the Boca Chica Viaduct. This bridge was completed in March 1911 and was 2,075 feet long, with 83 spandrel arches.

The Boca Chica Viaduct was a great experiment. All of the bridges prior to this one were made with imported sands and rock aggregate, materials that had to be purchased and hauled in by barge from long distances, and thus were expensive. In order to save money, the engineers experimented with the limestone rock near the Boca Chica site and found that they could make good concrete from the material with cement and seawater. This discovery changed the construction of the spandrel arches in another way—the engineers could not put steel reinforcing rod inside the arches because the salt would corrode the steel. As the steel rusted, it would cause spalling, the concrete would break up, and the arches would self-destruct. However, the engineers determined that for the low bridges like the Boca Chica span, steel reinforcing was not as necessary as it was for taller bridges. They built the Boca Chica Viaduct without steel and with local rock, setting a precedent that they used for all of the small arched bridges built after 1910.

The Boca Chica Viaduct was completely removed in the 1980s when the new highway was built. According to reports, the concrete was extremely good, and the contractor who broke up the bridge had great difficulty with the task because of the integrity of the viaduct.

Fig. 254. Tent Camp No. 18 on the grade on the west side of Boca Chica Key. Here again the roadbed was built by excavators on barges that dredged a canal on the side to get the fill for the grade. Photo is dated September 1907. (Jerry Wilkinson)

11
Stock Island and Key West

Stock Island

WORK BEGAN ON STOCK ISLAND in 1905, as it did elsewhere in the Keys. Because Stock Island was so close to Key West, it was easy to recruit local workers for this project. Again, it was a matter of men and mules, dynamite and wheelbarrows. The roadbed was finished on Stock Island in 1907. Two hundred workers lived at Camp 12, and their goal was to complete 50 feet of fill per day.

Key West

The town of Key West was the southernmost hub of the construction operation. This town, the largest and wealthiest city in Florida in 1890, was well situated to play a big role in the project because of the deep-water port it afforded. There was a large population of workers in Key West, and many of them migrated to the construction project because it was the biggest employer around.

But while there was deep water at Key West, there was not enough space for a major interna-

Fig. 255. Filling on Stock Island, looking to the southwest. Mules and carts moved the rock for the roadbed. (Museums at Crane Point Hammock)

Fig. 256. Camp No. 80 in Key West. Photo is dated February 24, 1906. (Museums at Crane Point Hammock)

tional terminal for Flagler's train. Thus the F.E.C. Construction Division began building land. Under the direction of Howard Trumbo, a great fill area was begun in 1906, and as time progressed, this terminal area grew to 134 acres. By 1916, dredging crews had moved 649,695 cubic yards of rock, 2,525,357 cubic yards of marl, and 6,119 cubic yards of sand and ballast to fill the terminal site and approach areas—a total of more than 3.1 million cubic yards of

material—almost 18 percent of the material moved for the railway project.

Trumbo first outlined the area for filling with large rock later hardened with concrete walls. The dredges found plenty of marl in the nearby bay bottom to place into the confines of these walls; this was a good place for orange peel dredge work. The fill area became known as Trumbo's Island and was later named Trumbo Point.

Dredges *George W. Allen* and *Grampus* did

Fig. 257. Dredges *George W. Allen* and *Grampus* in Key West. (Museums at Crane Point Hammock)

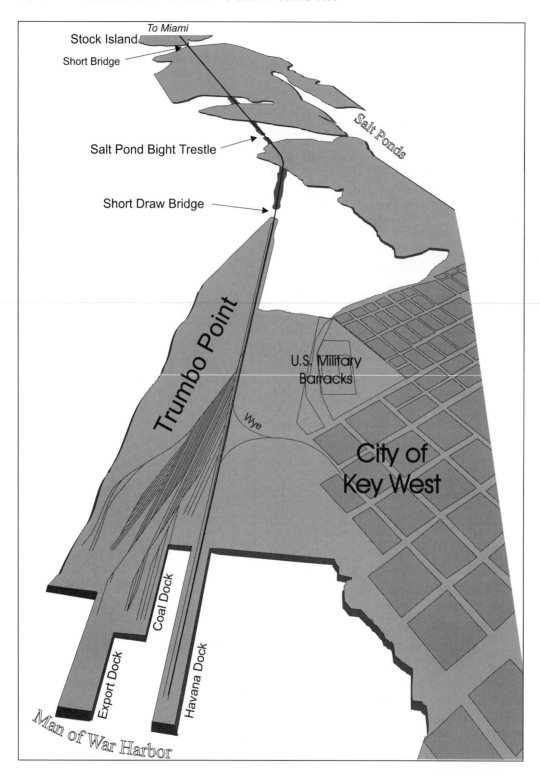

Fig. 259. Flyover of Trumbo Point and Key West.

most of the fill work at Trumbo Point. Both started in March 1906. The *George W. Allen* was not built by the F.E.C. but was purchased for the task. Once in place, these vessels worked around the clock with shift crews. In April 1907, the *George W. Allen* was out of service for a few

weeks when a steam pipe ruptured, killing two crewmen and injuring seven others. The vessel was relatively undamaged.

The main line of the Extension passed over Stock Island to Key West, then over the Salt Pond Bight Trestle. At MP 521 was a small

Fig. 259. View of Trumbo's Island looking up the right of way coming in from the east. Laborers have put down rudimentary working track. The city of Key West is on the right. Also note the shadow of the photographer in the foreground. (Monroe County Public Library)

Fig. 260. Trumbo's Island. Because all of the land was new, it appeared stark and barren. It was described as a "man-made desert." A cluster of tents is visible on the right. The superstructure of one of the dredges is visible in the center behind the building. The dredge is working in this photo; smoke is coming from the stack. (Monroe County Public Library)

drawbridge at the north end of Trumbo Point. Here there was an F.E.C. bridge tender's house, a toilet, and a water tank. Once on Trumbo Point, the track split into multiple sidings. The main destinations were the Havana Dock, the Coal Dock and the Export Dock, all with waterfront on Man of War Harbor. This was the dock configuration when completed in 1916. It was smaller when opened in 1912. There was no roundhouse at Key West. Trains turned on the wye south of the main line; this track led nearly into the city of Key West.

The U.S. military barracks housed both Army and Navy units. As Trumbo Point grew with continual filling operations, the military lost their waterfront property, and they would have lost all access to water if the drawbridge had not been installed.

The first dock completed at Key West

appears to have been the Havana Dock for passenger service. Early photos show this as a wooden dock; a concrete dock was built at a later date. An open passenger canopy extended for a couple of hundred feet between two tracks at the loading area.

The construction at Trumbo's Island and Key West began in 1905 and continued at a moderate pace until July 1907. *George W. Allen* and *Grampus* roared day and night on the north side of the town. On July 17, 1907, Meredith sent a telegram to the dredge crews to shut down their boilers. To the surprise and consternation of all of the businessmen and workers in Key West, the dredging and filling operations were curtailed by executive order of the F.E.C. This was Meredith's response to actions by the Naval Station in Key West, which was complaining about two perceived problems: the dredges were

Fig. 262. Another view of the wood dock at Key West. There is a train approaching the station and a steamer either approaching or leaving the dock in this photo. The dock is being widened; all of the structure from the train to the left is under construction. (Steele) (below)

Fig. 261. Original station dock at Key West. There are tracks on both sides of the terminal building canopy. The steamer on the right side of the dock is flying the Peninsular and Occidental Line flag; this was one of Flagler's fleet. (Steele)

taking marl from a location near Fleming Key (slated to be a torpedo boat base), and the filled causeways were hampering naval operations.

Earlier, Parrott and Meredith had worked out an agreement with the Navy that allowed the F.E.C. to take fill from the submerged area near tiny Fleming Key if the company put it back at some later time. When the Navy brought these negotiations in a completed contract to the table for signature, they included text to the effect that the F.E.C. must put the fill back on the other side of Fleming Key and make the key larger—a much more expensive proposition for the railroad. Thus Meredith—and especially Henry Flagler—were irate and closed the operations in Key West. Furthermore, the F.E.C. began shutting down camps in the lower Keys. Krome's formal statement follows: "Construction work of all kinds south of Knight's Key is to be suspended for an indefinite period, and as fast as

arrangements can be perfected to take care of the labor force at present between that point and Key West, all workmen will be transferred from this end of the line. A considerable portion of the plant and equipment now being used in the south will be moved north of Knight's Key and be placed in service there. The remainder will be put in shape to withstand a long lay-up, and left in charge of watchmen."

This news horrified the Key Westers. Rumors abounded that the railway would end at Bahia Honda (a possible deep-water port) or at Knight's Key, where the great Knight's Key Dock was soon to be a port. Flagler and Meredith gave no hint that they would reopen operations towards Key West but let the speculation continue.

Meredith had other reasons for shutting down the southern operation as well—the whole Construction Division was rushing to complete the line as far as Knight's Key so that they could

Fig. 263. New dock under construction at Key West. The wooden dock rail is visible on the far right. The workers are using a traveler that moves on rails to help them with the lifting work. The large barge in the center is a floating cement mixer. (Steele)

begin steamer operations as soon as possible. At this time (July 1907) the Long Key Viaduct was more than half completed, and there was a lot of work to be done through the upper and middle Keys, including finishing the roadbed and track from Conch Key through Vaca Key. Meredith needed manpower in the middle Keys. Nearly 1,000 lower Keys' workers were relocated to Long Key and to Knight's Key.

In the fall of 1907 many of the vessels were pulled from Key West and lower Keys' waters and sent up to Miami. Several were "mothballed" in the Miami River. In November the F.E.C. closed its Extension Office in Key West. In January 1908, when the track reached Knight's Key Dock, there were still no workers in the lower Keys, but rumors abounded that work would resume in March. In the spring workers were again sent down to the southern camps to begin the Bahia Honda Bridge and continue roadbed grading.

The affair with the Navy was actually a bold tactical maneuver on Meredith's part—he knew the citizens of Key West would bring political pressure on the Navy so that they would give in. Eventually the Navy backed down, and the dredges fired up their boilers and continued the Trumbo fill.

Key West also served as a major supply dump for

A SERIOUS SITUATION.

ALL WORK THIS SIDE OF KNIGHT'S KEY SUSPENDED.

Reasons for Company's Action Stated by Mr. Krome.

Fig. 264. Newspaper headline from the *Key West Citizen* dated July 18, 1907.

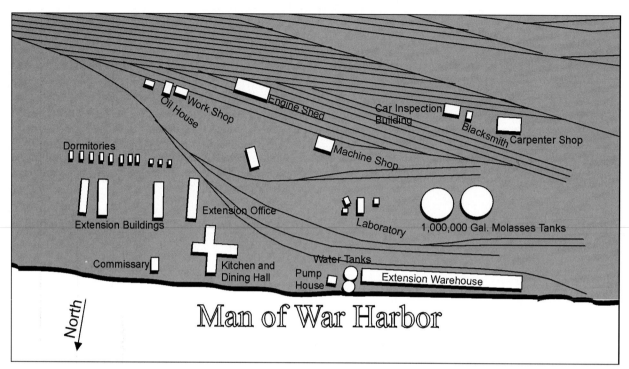

Oil House
Work Shop
Engine Shed
Car Inspection Building
Blacksmith
Carpenter Shop
Dormitories
Machine Shop
Extension Office
Laboratory
1,000,000 Gal. Molasses Tanks
Extension Buildings
Commissary
Kitchen and Dining Hall
Water Tanks
Pump House
Extension Warehouse

Man of War Harbor

North

Fig. 265. By 1916 there was an extensive operations complex on Trumbo Point on the bayside of the tracks. Amenities for the workers included a large kitchen/dining hall and dormitories. There was a large office building for the Extension management workers and an even larger warehouse. Scattered among the spur tracks were a machine shop, blacksmith shop, carpenter shop, workshop and a "drive-through" engine shed. Two huge tanks stored 1,000,000 gallons of molasses.

the Extension project. At the beginning of the project, engineers estimated that they would need 800,000 barrels of cement for all of the viaducts and piers. The cement was imported from Germany; the F.E.C. leased three oceangoing steamers to carry it. Thus it was important

that they bring the cement long before it was needed and then store it. Key West served as a major material storage depot very early in the project. By June 1906, all of the available space at the Mallory warehouses was full of cement, and another warehouse was built in Key West.

12

The Plan Revisited

The Extension Opens to Key West

ON THE MORNING OF January 21, 1912, engineers supervised workmen as they disassembled the 80-foot wooden trestle at Span 36 on the Knight's Key Bridge. Within a few hours they brought out the last two steel deck plates on barges, swung them into place, set the cross bracing, and began putting down ties and track over the final section of the Key West Extension. The agent and workers at the Knight's Key Dock Terminal closed up shop—there would no longer be rail/steamer service in the middle Keys. It was the last day before the Extension opened.

Fig. 266. Span No. 36 is closed. Unknown engineer poses for a photograph taken by W.R. Hawkins, who is standing on the Knight's Key Dock Trestle shooting to the north. (Monroe County Public Library)

175

Diarist W. R. Hawkins was there as an observer and photographer. This excerpt is from his journal:

January 21, 1912

I walked to K. K. Dock this A.M. I took some pictures of crossing (where Knight's Key Bridge crosses trestle) with girders in place. Took shot at Str. Montauk as she was leaving K. K. Dock. She carried R. H. Whitsall agent with his office and stevedore force and office fixtures and freight handling equipment to K. W. abandoning K. K. Dock as a station. I cast off her bow line from dock. Capt. Wm. Wagner with derrick barge #9 put up the last span (the crossing) this morning. A gang was at work riveting and another decking. The first train that ran the entire distance from Key West to Marathon came in tonight pulled by Eng. 12. Engineer Wm. Athern, W. J. Krome, C. S. Coe, McRae, Sheeran and others came on it.

January 22

Passenger train to Key West. Uncle Henry's train ran through to Key West this morning arriving at 10:55. I walked to K. K. dock this morning. It was showery.

I took a shot at "pilot train" Engine 12 and caboose which preceded Uncle H's train a few minutes. Also at U. H.'s but am afraid rain spoiled it. Uncle Henry's train was the first passenger train to cross the bridge.

Fig. 267. Hawkins "spoiled" shot of Henry Flagler's Extension Special as it passed over the now defunct Knight's Key Dock Trestle. In spite of the fact that Key West was apparently warm and sunny, it was raining in the middle Keys. (Monroe County Public Library)

Fig. 268. Work comes to a halt as Henry Flagler's train crosses Pigeon Key on its way to Key West. (Seth Bramson)

The train rolled on new shiny steel track over seven miles of water and through the lower Keys on its way to the southernmost city in the United States. It passed crews of workers as it sped along. Men with tired backs and calluses on their hands stopped their work, put down their tools, and waved and cheered as the train went by. While they may not have seen a glimpse of "Uncle Henry," they knew he was on board.

When the Extension Special rolled onto Trumbo's Island, young Marvin Thompson was waiting there in the crowd. He was 12 years old at the time, but well remembered the feelings and events. In 1967, he wrote an article of his impressions of that day:

> That first time, most of the population of Key West was there, too. Thousands were milling about Trumbo Island and Pablo Beach, impatiently comparing watches as zero hours of the Great Day drew near.
>
> Old Glory, the Cuban flag and other banners, streamers and bunting waved in the breeze at every vantage point. The Light-Guard Band was in good melody, as was the ever-popular "Phil Henson's Ragtime Family Band." Frankie Papy's entertainers always turned out when there was a need for special atmosphere and paraded with a martial air, flag flying, kettle drum ra-tat-tatting, base-

Fig. 269. With the skyline of Key West in the background, parades of citizens came to the newly created land on Trumbo's Island to celebrate the arrival of the first train.

drum booming, led by Dad with his flute and wearing his Uncle Sam suit with red and white tails and high top hat with white stars in a field of blue. Always their rendition of "Yankee Doodle" was great.

Many tents had been erected on the man-made desert that was Trumbo for the comfort of the thirsty and hungry throngs. Baked ham and pork sandwiches were consumed as fast as the church ladies could turn them out. Wooden wine barrels filled with Key lime juice mixed with sugar syrup and cooled with chunks of ice make a limeade that could not be equaled. Guava pie and fresh coconut ice cream also hit the spot. Other raters on the menu were turtle stew, crawfish enchilada and conch chowder, topped off with genuine Key lime pie.

Hordes of children accompanied their elders, all waving small American or Cuban flags and carrying bunches of roses and other flowers of many kinds and colors. Grandstand and bleachers resounded to their singing and laughing as they waited.

And now the atmosphere was rent by a sound such as Key West had never experienced before. It screeched and screamed like a trapped Everglades wildcat. It howled again from the swamps as it approached the Garrison Bight drawbridge, so that the bridge tender would make certain the span was safely closed. Finally the huge black monster slowed the steady grind of its drivers and entered upon the bridge, bell clanging, clouds of steam spewing and spraying, black smoke belching.

The Light-Guard Band was giving out with Dixie as the first train to enter Key West rolled majestically into the station area.

The Mayor and other dignitaries were ready and primed on the speakers stand, awaiting the arrival of Henry Flagler, the man who had just done more for Key West and Monroe County than any other person in their history.

A final burst of escaping steam, a clutching of brakes, a clashing together of steel coaches, a last ding-dong from the bell, a valedictory wildcat screech from the whistle, and the black dragon snorted and slid to a stop.

The welcoming committee lined up where the great man would walk to the speaker's stand. A moment of hushed watching and waiting, and then, as a form appeared in the doorway at the platform, deafening applause broke out. Friends stepped up on both sides of Flagler and took his hands and arms in theirs. Steps with red carpeting were placed. The Grand Old Man paused, smiled and asked, "Do I smell roses?" Indeed he did, for children had strewn their bouquets along the path to the speaker's stand.

After Mr. Flagler had been graciously received by the Mayor and other officials, celebration began on Trumbo Island, and elsewhere parades formed. As the day waned, the revelry waxed, and the quickened tempo spread to the Latin clubs. Their marimba bands formed a conga line in the city streets and swayed with the beat of the bongos. The club houses were gaily decorated inside and out with bunting and streamers, and the flags of both nations were displayed side by side as had been done for the many years since "El Grito de Yar," the clarion call for Cuban freedom. Steam whistles sounded at Consumer's Ice Plant, Columbia Laundry and the power plant of Stone and Webster. In the harbor tugs and steamships joined in.

This was January 22, 1912, a great day in the history of the Florida East Coast rail line, of its builder, Henry Flagler, of the citizens of Key West and of their neighbors to the south.

—Excerpt from *Key West Citizen*, March 6, 1967,
"The First and Last Trains." Reprinted with permission.

It was indeed a great day and a cause for celebration. Politicians and dignitaries basked in the sunshine of compliments and lofty speeches. The construction engineers and those responsible for the logistics of

Fig. 270. This low viaduct is probably one of the Saddle Bunch bridges. The earthen causeway to the right was the original temporary roadbed put in place in order to get the construction materials close to the job site. Workers have removed the track and piled the ties in stacks. This roadbed was clearly not suitable for passenger service, and would be easily washed out in even a minor hurricane. (Steele)

bringing together parts and materials from all over the world took great satisfaction in how well the plan worked. And the thousands of workers who built the Extension saw the fruit of their labors, and were proud that they had participated in the creation of a major engineering feat. Part of their job was over, part remained. They would soon be working to finish the Key West Extension.

Finishing the Extension

While the line was in place to Key West, the Key West Extension was far from complete. The 1912 right-of-way was very primitive and rudimentary and could very well have been termed the "First Extension." Most of it was rebuilt in the next four years. There was more construction activity in moving materials after January 1912 than before. Excavators and dredges worked day and night, adding mass and height to the roadbed. The roadbed was raised in many places by several feet, and it was widened and "hardened" by additional marl and riprap.

A number of the bridges were wooden trestles and were replaced by concrete viaducts before the line was finished. Most of the original track was replaced with heavier rail. In 1914 the laborers built seawalls from Bahia Honda to

West Summerland Key and at Long Key to protect the approaches from wave action. These walls are still visible today.

Marathon remained very active in this post-completion building process. It was still the center of F.E.C. activity as Krome and his staff oversaw the last stages of the project from the General Office building beside the Tail Track Dock until 1916. This was the period when Marathon matured as a town, with the remaining permanent staff building an athletic club, hosting tennis tournaments, and congealing as a community.

C. S. Coe still served as a major administrative engineer; he stayed with the F.E.C. in the Keys as Engineer, Maintenance of Way until 1917. His task was to oversee the rebuilding of the railway to make it as hurricane-proof as possible. As events would prove, Coe was remarkably successful.

Bridges

Bridge building was far from complete in 1912. Figures 271 and 272 are a bit daunting at first glance, but they show very well the pattern of bridge-building activity for the project. For the

Fig. 271. and 272. (Following two pages) Construction dates for the viaducts of the Key West Extension. These dates are from the Annual Construction Reports filed by the F.E.C., courtesy of research by Bill Robinson.

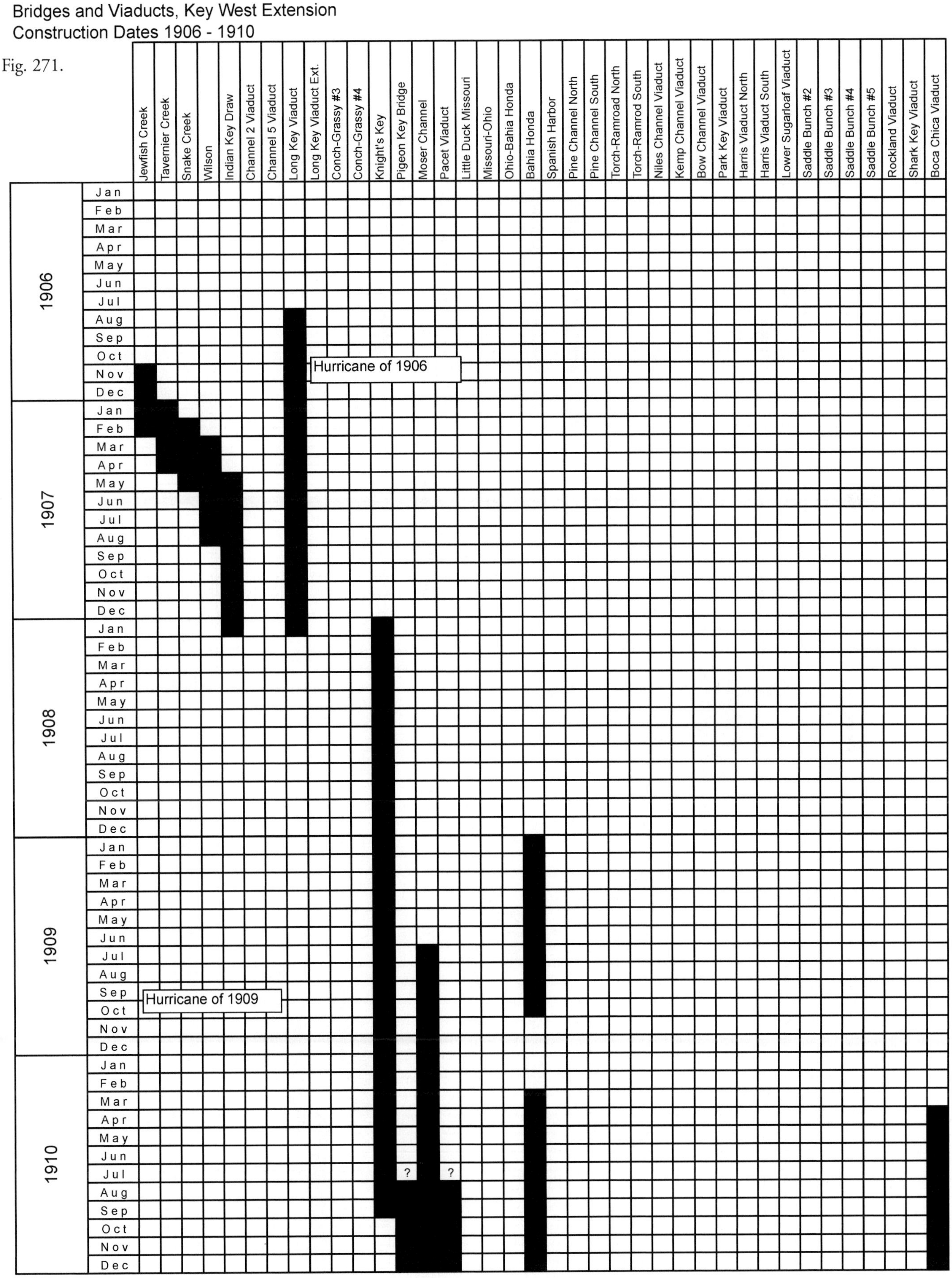

Bridges and Viaducts, Key West Extension
Construction Dates 1906 - 1910

Fig. 271.

Column headers: Jewfish Creek · Tavernier Creek · Snake Creek · Wilson · Indian Key Draw · Channel 2 Viaduct · Channel 5 Viaduct · Long Key Viaduct · Long Key Viaduct Ext. · Conch-Grassy #3 · Conch-Grassy #4 · Knight's Key · Pigeon Key Bridge · Moser Channel · Pacet Viaduct · Little Duck Missouri · Missouri-Ohio · Ohio-Bahia Honda · Bahia Honda · Spanish Harbor · Pine Channel North · Pine Channel South · Torch-Ramrod North · Torch-Ramrod South · Niles Channel Viaduct · Kemp Channel Viaduct · Bow Channel Viaduct · Park Key Viaduct · Harris Viaduct North · Harris Viaduct South · Lower Sugarloaf Viaduct · Saddle Bunch #2 · Saddle Bunch #3 · Saddle Bunch #4 · Saddle Bunch #5 · Rockland Viaduct · Shark Key Viaduct · Boca Chica Viaduct

Row years: 1906, 1907, 1908, 1909, 1910 (each with months Jan–Dec)

Hurricane of 1906

Hurricane of 1909

?   ?

Bridges and Viaducts, Key West Extension
Construction Dates 1911 - 1915

Fig. 272.

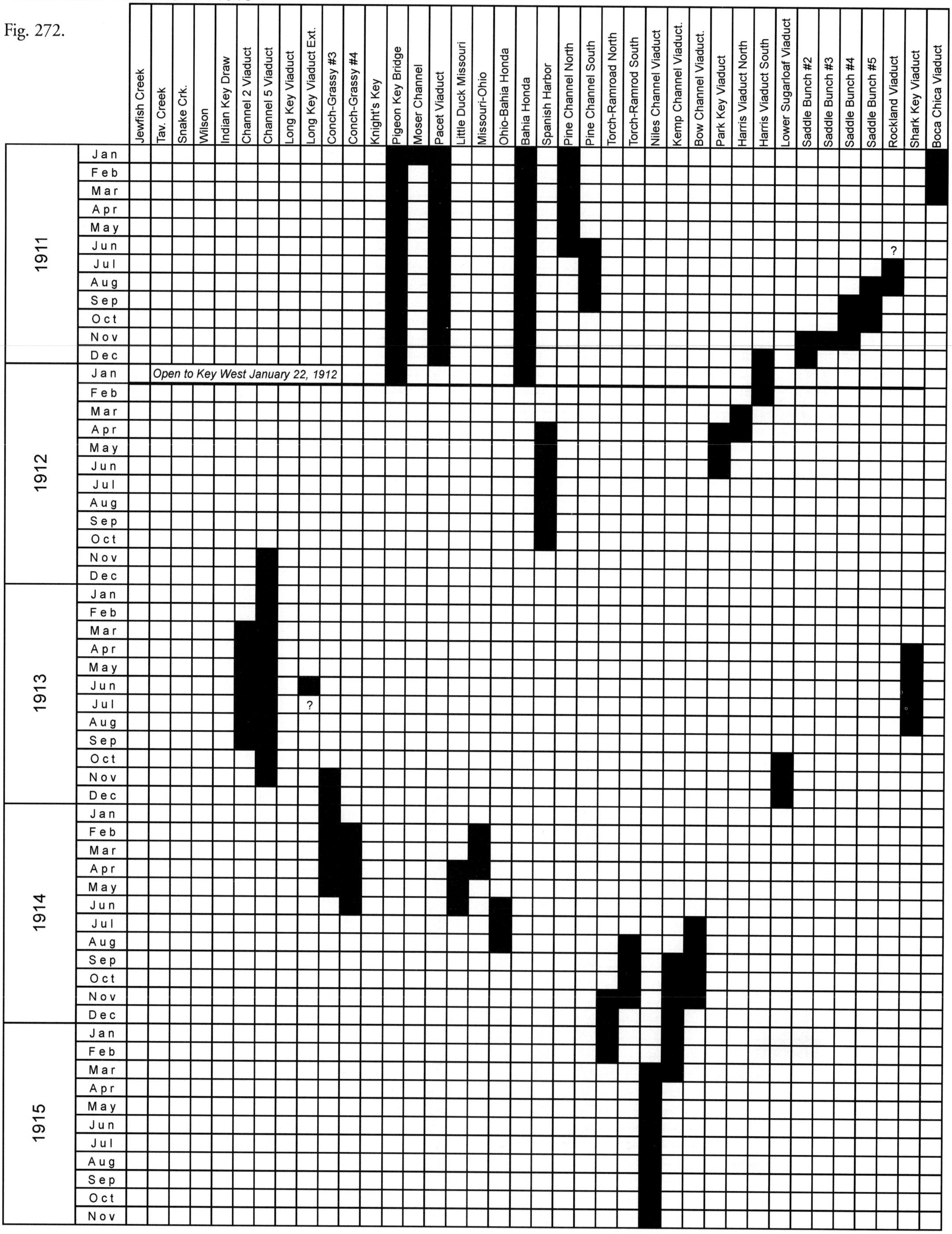

Column headers (left to right):

Jewfish Creek · Tav. Creek · Snake Crk. · Wilson · Indian Key Draw · Channel 2 Viaduct · Channel 5 Viaduct · Long Key Viaduct · Long Key Viaduct Ext. · Conch-Grassy #3 · Conch-Grassy #4 · Knight's Key · Pigeon Key Bridge · Moser Channel · Pacet Viaduct · Little Duck Missouri · Missouri-Ohio · Ohio-Bahia Honda · Bahia Honda · Spanish Harbor · Pine Channel North · Pine Channel South · Torch-Ramrod North · Torch-Ramrod South · Niles Channel Viaduct · Kemp Channel Viaduct. · Bow Channel Viaduct. · Park Key Viaduct · Harris Viaduct North · Harris Viaduct South · Lower Sugarloaf Viaduct · Saddle Bunch #2 · Saddle Bunch #3 · Saddle Bunch #4 · Saddle Bunch #5 · Rockland Viaduct · Shark Key Viaduct · Boca Chica Viaduct

Row groups (years with months Jan–Dec):
1911 (Jan–Dec)
1912 (Jan–Dec) — *Open to Key West January 22, 1912*
1913 (Jan–Dec)
1914 (Jan–Dec)
1915 (Jan–Nov)

Annotations: "?" markers at Rockland Viaduct (1911 Jun/Jul), Channel 5 Viaduct (1913 Jul), and Shark Key Viaduct (1913 Jul).

first two years, the major bridges of concern were those that put the track down to Marathon. Two of the water crossings were on trestles (Channel 2 and Channel 5); these were later bridged with concrete viaducts (see Fig. 139, page 95). During the next four years concentration was on the remaining big water crossings—the Knight's Key to Little Duck Key bridge and the Bahia Honda Bridge, which were essential for the run to Key West. During this second period, some other smaller viaducts were installed, notably the Saddle Bunch Viaducts and the Boca Chica Viaduct. This latter bridge was very important; it provided a route to send supplies and materials northward from Key West.

After the January 22, 1912, opening, bridge building appeared to taper off for a few months; there were crews working only in the lower Keys at the time. Beginning in 1913, a flurry of bridge building resumed, with construction of the Channel 2 and Channel 5 viaducts in the upper Keys. It appears that over the next two years, the company allocated its resources to build bridges from the upper Keys downward.

The workers became quite proficient at building the spandrel arches. Some of the bridges, notably the short viaducts in the Saddle Bunches, were completed in only a month. These bridges were not as complex as those in deep water, and they were accessible with rail lines bringing supplies from Key West. The same crews jumped from one site to the next, continuing the northward progress with the same tools and forms used over and over again.

Deviations from the Plan

Fortunately, Meredith's grand plan included a major point: Be flexible. Without this inclusion, the Extension might have cost much more to build, may have been more prone to disaster in hurricanes, and may have been much delayed in its completion. In retrospect, the entire Extension project went according to Meredith's plan, with a couple of major exceptions where the engineers and management made good decisions to deviate from the plan.

There were minor changes to the plan early in the construction process. Lake Surprise, for example, did not show up on the initial surveyor's reports, and, as a result, took considerable effort and time to fill with a causeway in 1906. In a way this was beneficial—it gave the excavator crews a chance to hone their skills for the

Fig. 273. Building the additional causeway at Surprise Lake. (Museums at Crane Point Hammock)

future tasks they would face.

The hurricanes of 1906 changed plans in two major ways. With the deaths of the hundred workers on Quarterboat 4 at Long Key, management determined that they would minimize quarterboats and build more substantial land-based camps. If they used quarterboats, they built protected canals for them and mandated that workers evacuate from quarterboats if hurricanes threatened.

These hurricanes also demonstrated that it was not as safe to use fill in between the Keys, as they had initially hoped. The sand fill was especially vulnerable to washing out, even when buttressed with riprap. Consequently, they built more bridges than they planned, rather than minimize the number. They also "hardened" most of the causeways with additional marl.

In some cases they made existing bridges longer to increase water flow between the keys. The Long Key Viaduct was supposed to comprise 180 arches with a long fill approach on the western end. After the 1909 hurricane, and with the massive water flow that passed through the crossing, the engineers added 35 arches instead of filling in the approach. Today this change in

the plan is still visible; there is a great wing-wall abutment standing alone in the channel, 1,512 feet west of Long Key. This additional construction began in June 1913 and was completed in a couple of months.

The spandrel arches throughout the Keys were initially meant to be built with steel reinforcing rod inside the concrete. The Long Key Viaduct was done in this fashion. However, this added much to the work, and the engineers were not sure that the steel would last in a salt-water environment. Using steel mandated that all of the concrete be mixed with only fresh water—another expensive commodity. So, as noted in Chapter 10, they deviated from the plan, beginning with the Boca Chica Viaduct in 1910, and found that the local rock mixed with cement and seawater made good concrete. All of the remaining spandrel bridges were built this way, which saved considerable money.

The greatest deviation from the original plan was the connection from Knight's Key to Little Duck Key. The final bridge that spanned this crossing was radically different from the original proposed by Meredith in 1905. The original plan for this long crossing was to build approximately

Fig. 274. Reinforcing steel rods in the spandrel arch lower sections. While this added to the strength of the bridge and helped tie the components together, the rods were prone to rusting. (Monroe County Public Library)

Fig. 275. The Long Key Bridge Extension begins at the wing wall abutment at the right and carries 35 arches to the final abutment in the distance. (Photo by author, 2001.)

four miles of rock embankment over shallow areas. The planners would then bridge the deeper waters with two concrete arch bridges, such as those on the Long Key Viaduct. Figure 276 shows that the northernmost arch span was to stretch from the abutment at Knight's Key and course westward 7,300 feet towards Pigeon Key. At this point the arches would terminate at an abutment that would be the beginning of filled causeway, which would extend to Pigeon Key, then pass over it and beyond to a second abutment about half a mile west of Pigeon Key. The entire space between the abutments was to be covered with an elevated fill causeway made from rock and marl. This causeway would have been about 30 feet high at each abutment, would dip as it passed over Pigeon Key, then would rise again at the western abutment. The total length of this fill would be 5,940 feet, or about 1.13 miles. From this westernmost abutment, the second bridge would extend 7,800 feet farther towards Little Duck Key. This section of bridge would end with a third abutment and then continue as elevated rock fill for the remaining three miles to Little Duck Key.

The master plan for the seven-mile crossing was changed sometime in 1909 for numerous reasons. The original plan was to build the entire extension with concrete arched bridges because long-term maintenance costs for concrete bridges would be much less than with steel construction. However, the great concrete bridge at Long Key turned out to be more difficult and expensive to build than anticipated. Furthermore, the whole Extension project was behind schedule, and a steel bridge would go up faster than the arches.

In 1905, at the beginning of the project, it was more cost-effective to build bridges with concrete rather than steel, but with changes in U.S. steel production, the costs of building a steel bridge dropped somewhat in the latter part of the decade. One other factor figured into the design change—the hurricane of 1906 showed that fill was vulnerable to washout. The original design had 4.3 miles of rock fill, and this may have made the entire crossing fail in a major hurricane. Bridges were safer than fill.

The construction team under Krome thus dropped the original plan and redesigned the whole crossing to the present-day configuration. As seen in Figure 277, the final seven-mile-long bridge had no rock fill but was built with 1.8 miles of spandrel arches and 5.1 miles of steel deck plate spans on tall piers. In addition, they constructed a swing bridge at Moser Channel

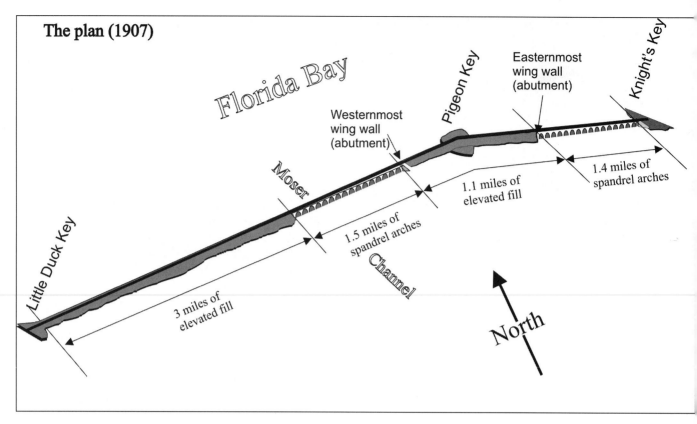

Fig. 276. The original plan for the seven-mile crossing with the extensive causeway in the middle and two long viaducts.

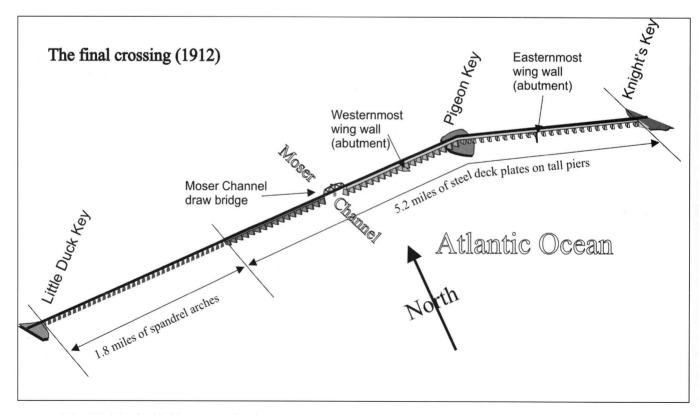

Fig. 277. The final bridge as completed in 1912.

Fig. 278. View of the wing wall today. It is noticeably shorter with the upper portion removed. (Photo by author.)

Fig. 279. Part of the cut-off abutment lies on the floor of Florida Bay, and is easily visible from the Seven-Mile Bridge. (Photo by author.)

that was not in the original plan.

Steel spans were ordered for the great bridge in March 1909, but not before the workers had begun to build the original bridge. The vestigial beginnings of the original plan are still standing—the two wing wall abutments for the Pigeon Key causeway were completed as the first stage of the project. However, the abutments, designed to be the termination points for the ends of the causeway, were too tall for the revised construction plan with steel deck plates.

Thus they were chopped off, and the upper portions were dropped into the shallow waters of Florida Bay, where they can still be seen as a remnant of the original plans.

End of the Key West Extension

In September 1935 a great hurricane hit the middle and upper areas of the Florida Keys. According to folklore, this Labor Day Hurricane destroyed the railroad and Henry Flagler's dream, and those who had once decried the roadway as

Fig. 280. View from Pigeon Key looking west in early 1909. The viewer is on a high vantage point (the cement warehouse roof) looking at the abutment about half a mile away. There are no piers yet, but there is a temporary trestle that would have been used to bring in fill for the causeway. Note the triangular shape inside the inset square. This is the abutment that was to be the terminal point for the fill on the western end. It was built before any piers and was later cut down when the engineers decided to use steel deck plate construction. (Wright Langley Archives)

"Flagler's Folly" probably said, "I told you so."

But did the Labor Day Hurricane destroy the Key West Extension? Storm surge came ashore in the Matecumbe Keys and Windley Key; the water was reportedly 18 feet above high tide. The force was strong enough to wash several coaches and boxcars off the track on lower Matecumbe Key, although it left the engine upright. Several miles of railroad track were twisted like pretzels by the force, and some of the fill was washed away.

The rest of the railway roadbed was intact. It was rebuildable. In fact, the F.E.C. replaced the dam-aged track within a couple of months in order to bring the valuable cars and engine back to Miami.

None of the bridges were damaged by the storm. No approaches were washed out, no sections displaced from any of the steel bridges, no spandrel arches breeched. Most of the marl-reinforced roadbed survived the most intense storm of the twentieth century to hit the U.S. Meredith's designs, and Krome's and Coe's execution of these plans, proved to be a match for the great force of Mother Nature. In fact, none of the original bridges have ever been destroyed or damaged by any force other than man.

Fig. 281. Automobile ferry in use for the run between lower Matecumbe Key and Grassy Key. (Monroe County Public Library)

Why was the Extension not rebuilt? There are a number of good reasons. The F.E.C. was in receivership at the time and not in a position to put much money into repairs. The U.S. was in the grip of the Depression; times were tight all over. But in some respects, the Key West Extension died because it was a dinosaur even as it was being built in the 1910s. In the late 1800s, rail lines connected the U.S. to move people and commodities; there was no vision of doing business any other way. By the turn of the century, and certainly by the 1920s, a whole new mode of transportation evolved—the automobile. People no longer wanted to take trains, they wanted to drive.

Highways and roads began to crisscross the country. The pressure to build roads was everywhere, even in the Keys. By 1928, a road and ferry system was in place that allowed drivers to get to Key West on the first Overseas Highway. The ferry portion covered 40 miles from lower Matecumbe Key to No Name Key. In 1930, this trip was reduced to 14 over-water miles when a highway was put in from Grassy Key to the west end of Marathon. In 1933, the Florida Legislature created the Overseas Road and Toll Bridge District to complete a highway from lower Matecumbe Key to Big Pine Key to eliminate the ferries. This would have competed with the Extension service.

Construction for a major highway bridge below lower Matecumbe Key was just beginning

Fig. 282. One of the wooden highway bridges built in 1934. The railroad right-of-way is to the right. (Monroe County Public Library)

in August 1935. Workers completed eight of the piers for this bridge to parallel the railroad right-of-way. The Labor Day Hurricane blew the project to a halt; of the 400 workers in the Keys, an estimated 259 died in the storm surge. All of their equipment was destroyed. Today visitors still ask questions about the big blocks that they see on the bay side at lower Matecumbe—these are the remains of those first concrete highway piers.

In some ways this great storm was fortuitous for the F.E.C. and for those who wanted a highway to Key West. Because of the great expense of building it and maintaining it, the Extension line was allowed to charge premium rates for service and freight but was in all likelihood losing money. After the hurricane, the company petitioned the federal court for authority to abandon the line rather than rebuild it, and it was so granted. This decision opened the way for the Overseas Road and Toll Bridge District, the State of Florida, and Monroe County to purchase all of the bridges and right-of-way. They did so as quickly as possible; the old bridges were the key to the new Overseas Highway. The F.E.C. netted $640,000 for the Key West Extension, much less than the estimated $50,000,000 that it cost them to build it in the 1910s. The highway groups got a real bargain: a well-developed right-of-way for the second Overseas Highway. This one lasted until the late 1970s/early 1980s, when the present road was built on top of the old highway. The state put in all new bridges but left all of the railroad filled causeways in place, then added much more fill to raise them higher and make them wider.

Many of the old bridges were left in place. Others were partially dismantled. They serve as pedestrian or fishing bridges, and they have a bright future as part of a Keys-wide network of alternative transportation pathways.

The new highway thus grew from the bones of the Extension dinosaur. So, as you drive your motor vehicle—rental car, SUV, motorcycle or conch cruiser—down the Keys today, notice the bridges that you pass on your way. They were built nearly a hundred years ago when this chain of islands was much different than it is today. Be aware that 22 miles of your trip is over land that was underwater in 1905, and 18 miles of your passage is over water—in all, 40 miles of created structure superimposed on the natural keys. Pay attention to the segues in the road that you drive at each of the transitions from new bridge to highway. You will find that most of your trip from Homestead to Key West is on the ancient roadbed of the great Key West Extension. The rock beneath your tires was first put in place by strong men long gone from this Earth, who came to the Keys to make a living with their muscles and vigor. These were common men who bought into Henry Flagler's dream, who dumped a wheelbarrow of broken rock on a wet spot, then turned around to do it again.

On your drive, stop now and then at one of the abandoned bridges. Take a walk on it. Look down on the mighty mangroves that are attempting to reclaim the roadbed. The mangroves have a daunting task—Meredith's bridges and Flagler's Folly of the Key West Extension may endure a thousand years. Enjoy your ride.

References

THIS BOOK WAS MEANT to be readable, and I have not included footnotes with every sentence. All of the facts on which the story is based have been verified by at least two primary sources. A list of primary sources and suggestions for further reading follows.

Most of the material in this book comes from the sources and materials cited. There are, however, some new materials not previously published that require specific documentation and citation. They include the following pages and passages:

Chapter 2, pages 25–27. While it is well known that there were remote marl pits located at some distance from the main line, these stories have not been documented with photographs. Thanks to the pictures contributed by Louis "Pete" Bow, we have a more complete understanding of how the marl-handling operations worked. Interpretations of the photos are mine.

Chapter 10, pages 149–152. This is entirely new material on the Bahia Honda Bridge. Figure 226 and the theory of construction progress are largely derived from Figure 225 and my own observations.

Chapter 12, pages 185–188. While it has been generally understood that the wing wall abutments at Pigeon Key and at the Long Key Viaduct were intended to be terminal walls for causeways, until the present time there were no conclusive documents proving this. Figures 278, 279, and 280 on pages 187–188, along with the F.E.C. Annual Reports and orders for steel stand as strong proof that the original bridge was modified dramatically from the original plan.

Adams, O. Burton. "Construction of Florida's Overseas Railway." *Apalachee*, Vol. 7, Tallahassee, FL: Tallahassee Historical Society, 1970.

Blair, Fredrick. "Railroad Creeps Out to Sea." *The Technical World Magazine*, 1907, pp. 484-88.

Bramson, Seth. *Speedway to Sunshine*. Erin, Ontario: The Boston Mills Press, 1984.

Clupper, Jim. *Index to Florida Times-Union Articles on the Upper Keys.* Monroe County Public Library, Helen Wadley Branch, Islamorada, FL.

Corliss, Carlton. "Building the Overseas Railway to Key West." *Tequesta*, No. 13, 1953, pp. 3-21.

—. "The Iron Horse in the Florida Keys." *Tequesta*, No. 29, 1969, pp. 17-26.

—. Miscellaneous original notes and correspondence in the collection of Wright Langley, Key West, FL

Dean, Love. "Heading South, Part 1." *Florida Keys Magazine*, Spring 1982, pp. 31ff.

—. "Heading South, Part 2." *Florida Keys Magazine*, Summer 1982, pp. 38ff.

Eggleston, Howard. "Florida East Coast Railway—Key West Extension. Part 2. Roadbed Construction." *Engineering-Contracting*, Vol. 28, No. 14, October 2, 1907.pp. 202-203.

—. "Florida East Coast Railway—Key West Extension. Part 3: Temporary Trestle Work." *Engineering-Contracting*, Vol. 28, No. 19, October 16, 1907, pp. 227-28.

—. "Florida East Coast Railway—Key West Extension. Part 4. Concrete Construction." *Engineering-Contracting*, Vol. 28, No. 19, November 6, 1907, pp. 264-66.

Eyster, Irving and Jeanne. *Islamorada and More.* Pigeon Key Foundation, 1997.

Gallagher, Dan. *Pigeon Key and the Seven-Mile Bridge.* Pigeon Key Foundation, 1995.

—. "Building the Old Bridges of the Florida Keys." In Gallagher (ed.), *The Florida Keys Environmental Story*, Monroe County Environmental Education Advisory Council, 1997, pp. 145-48.

—. *Marathon: Heart of the Key West Extension.* Pigeon Key Foundation, 1999.

"Great Ocean Railway, Florida to Key West." *Popular Mechanics*, Vol. 10, No. 2, February 1908, pp. 70-72.

Hawkins, W. R. Journal kept from March 5, 1909, to September 14, 1912. In archives of Henry Morrison Flagler Museum, Palm Beach, FL. Copy in possession of author.

Paine, Ralph D. "Over the Florida Keys by Rail." *Everybody's Magazine*, Vol. 18, No. 2, February, 1908, pp. 147-56.

Patterson, Frank. "The Florida East Coast Railway Key West Extension." *Railway Age Gazette*, May 10, 1912.

Pyfrom, Priscilla Coe. *The Bridges Stand Tall.* Pigeon Key Foundation, 1998.

Tinkham, Todd. "The Florida East Coast Extension." Unpublished thesis, Kalamazoo College, 1968.

Viele, John. "Key Vaca and Marathon." In Gallagher (ed.), *The Florida Keys Environmental Story,* Monroe County Environmental Education Advisory Council, 1997, pp. 85-86.

Wilkinson, Jerry. "Building the Overseas Railroad. Assorted Florida East Coast Railway Equipment," preserved by William J. Krome and the Krome family. Compiled and bound, 1995.

—"Building the Overseas Railroad." Newspaper clippings, February 1909 to December 1909, preserved by William J. Krome and the Krome family. Compiled and bound, 1995.

—"Building the Overseas Railroad." Newspaper clippings, October 1905 to December 1906, preserved by William J. Krome and the Krome family. Compiled and bound, 1995.

—"Building the Overseas Railroad." Newspaper clippings, December 1906 to June 1907, preserved by William J. Krome and the Krome family. Compiled and bound, 1995.

—"Building the Overseas Railroad." Newspaper clippings, 1907, preserved by William J. Krome and the Krome family. Compiled and bound, 1995.

Index

If you enjoyed reading this book, here are some other books from Pineapple Press on related topics. For a complete catalog, write to Pineapple Press, P.O. Box 3889, Sarasota, FL 34230 or call 1-800-PINEAPL (746-3275). Or visit our website at www.pineapplepress.com.

The Florida Keys by John Viele. The trials and successes of the Keys pioneers are brought to life in this series, which recounts tales of early pioneer life and life at sea. **Volume 1**: *A History of the Pioneers* ISBN 1-56164-101-4 (hb); **Volume 2**: *True Stories of the Perilous Straits* ISBN 1-56164-179-0 (hb); **Volume 3**: *The Wreckers* ISBN 1-56164-219-3 (hb)

Lighthouses of the Florida Keys by Love Dean. Intriguing, well-researched accounts of the shipwrecks, construction mishaps, natural disasters, and Indian attacks that plagued the Florida Keys' lighthouses and their keepers. ISBN 1-56164-160-X (hb); 1-56164-165-0 (pb)

Over Key West and the Florida Keys by Charles Feil. A gorgeous color album featuring aerial photographs of islands large and small, glistening waters, and serene communities. Captions provide bits of Keys history. ISBN 1-56164-240-1 (hb)

Houses of Key West by Alex Caemmerer. Eyebrow houses, shotgun houses, Conch Victorians, and many more styles illustrated with lavish color photographs and complemented by anecdotes about old Key West. ISBN 1-56164-009-3 (pb)

Hemingway's Key West Second Edition by Stuart McIver. A rousing, true-to-life portrait of Hemingway in Key West, Cuba, and Bimini during his heyday. Includes a two-hour walking tour of the author's favorite Key West haunts and a narrative of the places he frequented in Cuba. ISBN 1-56164-241-X (pb)

Key West Gardens and Their Stories by Janis Frawley-Holler. Venture off the beaten track and enjoy beautiful views of the islanders' sanctuaries as well as fascinating stories and histories of the grounds where gardens now grow. Full color throughout. ISBN 1-56164-204-5 (pb)

The Florida Chronicles by Stuart B. McIver. A series offering true-life sagas of the notable and notorious characters throughout history who have given Florida its distinctive flavor. **Volume 1**: *Dreamers, Schemers and Scalawags* ISBN 1-56164-155-3 (pb); **Volume 2**: *Murder in the Tropics* ISBN 1-56164-079-4 (hb); **Volume 3**: *Touched by the Sun* ISBN 1-56164-206-1 (hb)

Florida Portrait by Jerrell Shofner. Packed with hundreds of photos, this word-and-picture album traces the history of Florida from the Paleo-Indians to the rampant growth of the late twentieth century. ISBN 1-56164-121-9 (pb)

Florida's Past Volumes 1, 2, and 3 by Gene Burnett. Collected essays from Burnett's "Florida's Past" columns in *Florida Trend* magazine, plus some original writings not found elsewhere. Burnett's easygoing style and his sometimes surprising choice of topics make history good reading. **Volume 1** ISBN 1-56164-115-4 (pb); **Volume 2** ISBN 1-56164-139-1 (pb); **Volume 3** ISBN 1-56164-117-0 (pb)

Key Biscayne by Joan Gill Blank. This engaging history of the southernmost barrier island in the U.S. tells the stories of its owners and would-be owners. ISBN 1-56164-096-4 (hb); 1-56164-103-0 (pb)